UNIT E

Weather and Climate

Theme: Constancy and Change

THINK LIKE A SCIENTIST

TORNADO WARNING

Tornadoes, such as this one seen over a Texas prairie, can have wind speeds up to 500 km/h. Tornadoes are the most violent storms on Earth. Hundreds of tornadoes strike the United States each year. Scientists study actual tornadoes, measuring conditions that occur within them. Artificial tornadoes are also studied in laboratory experiments. Yet, scientists still don't fully understand how tornadoes develop.

Do a Test • Record and Analyze • Draw Conclusions • Make Observations • Ask a Question • Make a Hypothesis • Plan and Do a Test

Ask a Question • Make a Hypothesis • Plan and Do a Test • Record and Analyze • Draw Conclusio

THINK LIKE A SCIENTIST

Questioning In this unit you'll study tornadoes and other types of storms. You'll investigate questions such as these.

- What Is Air Pressure?
- What Can Clouds Tell You About the Weather?

Observing, Testing, Hypothesizing In the Activity "Tornado Tube," you'll make observations about the motion of swirling water. You'll also hypothesize about the motion of air in a tornado.

Researching In the Resource "The Fiercest Storms on Earth," you'll gather more information about the nature of tornadoes, and hurricanes too!

Drawing Conclusions After you've completed your investigations, you'll draw conclusions about what you've learned— and get new ideas.

THE AIR AROUND US

What do you need air for? You need it to breathe, of course. But is air important for anything else? Learning about air is a good way to begin learning about something that affects you every day. That something is weather.

PEOPLE USING SCIENCE

Meteorologist On Sunday, March 11, 1888, a storm stalled over New York City, dumping 53 cm (21 in.) of snow. Wind gusts of 117 km/h (73 mph) piled up 6-m (20-ft) high snowdrifts, stranding New Yorkers in trains and horse-drawn carriages. There had been no warning that a major blizzard was coming. People lost their lives.

On January 7 and January 8, of 1996, almost 70 cm (28 in.) of snow fell on New York City. For that storm, meteorologists (mēt ē ər äl'ə jists) such as Al Roker were able to give people lots of warning. A meteorologist is a scientist who studies the atmosphere and forecasts the weather. Thanks to meteorologists, New Yorkers were spared tragedies like those suffered in the Blizzard of 1888.

Coming Up

◄ Meteorologist Al Roker not only forecasts the weather but has fun announcing his forecasts on television.

WHAT IS AIR?

Suppose someone asked you to describe the air. Perhaps you'd say, "Air is something that makes your hair blow on a windy day." But what is that "something"? In Investigation 1 you'll find out.

Activity

An Empty Cup

If you had a cup filled with hot chocolate, would you say that the cup is empty? Of course not. But what if you were to drink all the hot chocolate? Would the cup be empty then? Find out!

MATERIALS

- large clear plastic bowl
- water
- plastic-foam peanut
- clear plastic cup
- clear plastic cup with small hole
- *Science Notebook*

SAFETY

Clean up spills immediately.

Procedure

1. Fill a clear bowl with water. Float a plastic-foam peanut in it.

2. **Talk with your group** and together **predict** what will happen to the peanut if you cover it with a clear plastic cup and then push the cup under the water to the bottom of the bowl. **Write** your prediction in your *Science Notebook*. **Draw** a picture to show your prediction.

Step 1

3. **Test** your prediction. Turn a cup upside down and push it *straight down* over the peanut until the rim of the cup touches the bottom of the bowl. **Record** what happens to the peanut.

Step 4

4. Repeat step 3, using a clear plastic cup that has a small hole in its side, near the base. **Record** your observations.

Analyze and Conclude

1. **Compare** your results in step 3 with your prediction. What happened to the peanut? Write a **hypothesis** to explain why this happened. Give reasons to support your thoughts.

2. What happened to the peanut in step 4? **Hypothesize** why this happened. Based on this hypothesis, **predict** what would happen if you were to cover the hole with a finger or piece of tape and then repeat the experiment.

3. Was the cup empty or not? Explain your answer. What can you **infer** about air from this activity?

INVESTIGATE FURTHER!

EXPERIMENT

Use a straw to blow air into the bottom of the bowl of water you used in this activity. Blow as hard and as steadily as you can. Have a partner observe what happens to the level of the water in the bowl as you blow into the straw. Infer what's causing a change in water level.

Activity

An Ocean of Air

Have you ever gone swimming in the ocean? Can you remember the feeling of water pressing against you? In this activity you'll find out about the "ocean" that presses against you on dry land!

MATERIALS
- goggles
- thin wooden slats
- newspaper
- scissors
- *Science Notebook*

SAFETY
Wear goggles during this activity.

Procedure

1. Lay a wooden slat across your desk so that about one half of the slat hangs over the edge of the desktop.

 Math Hint *To find the midpoint of the wooden slat, measure the length of the slat. Divide that measurement by 2.*

Step 2

2. Use the palm of your hand to strike down on the end of the slat that is hanging over. **Record** what happens in your *Science Notebook*. Then put the slat back in the same position as before.

3. Place a sheet of newspaper over the part of the slat that is on the desk. Strike the slat as you did in step 2. **Record** your observations.

Step 3

4. Place a slat on the desk in the same position you placed it in step 1. Cut the newspaper in half. Lay one half of the paper over the part of the slat that is on the desk. With other group members, **predict** what will happen when you strike the slat this time. **Record** your prediction and then test it. Be sure to strike the slat as you did in step 2. **Record** your observations.

Step 4

Analyze and Conclude

1. **Compare** what you observed in step 2 with what you observed in step 3. **Describe** the difference in your results.

2. **Describe** what happened in step 4. How does it **compare** with your prediction?

3. Think about what was holding down the newspaper when you struck the slat in step 3. **Infer** whether that same "thing" was holding down the half sheet of newspaper in step 4. Do you think this "thing" has weight? Give reasons for your answer.

Technology Link CD-ROM

INVESTIGATE FURTHER!

Use the **Science Processor CD-ROM**, *Weather and Climate* (Investigation 1, Up, Up, and Away) to take an imaginary weather-balloon ride. Find out about the layers of the atmosphere. Ride the balloon higher and higher to learn which gases you'll find at each layer.

It's Got Us Covered

Reading Focus What gases make up air, and how do they make life possible?

▲ Air is matter, just as all of the objects shown are matter.

You feel it when a gentle breeze touches your face. You hear it rustling leaves. You see its force bend tree branches. What is this thing that hints of its presence but is tasteless, odorless, and unseen? It's the air.

It's a Mix of Matter

Air is made up of matter. Like objects that you can see, air takes up space and has weight. The activity on pages E6 and E7 shows that air takes up space. When the cup was pushed down over the plastic-foam peanut, the water did not rise to fill the cup. That's because the cup was already filled with air. The activity on pages E8 and E9 demonstrates the effect of the weight of air when a wooden slat covered with newspaper is struck. The weight of the air holds the newspaper down over the slat as it is struck.

Air is a mixture of gases. Like all matter, these gases are made up of tiny particles that are in constant motion.

The circle graph on the next page shows the mixture of gases that make up air. The largest part of air is made up of **nitrogen** (nī′trə jən). The second most plentiful gas is **oxygen** (äks′i jən). The small portion of air that's left is made up of other gases, including **carbon dioxide** (kär′bən dī äks′īd) and **water vapor**.

Is the amount of nitrogen in Earth's air closer to $\frac{1}{2}$ or $\frac{3}{4}$?

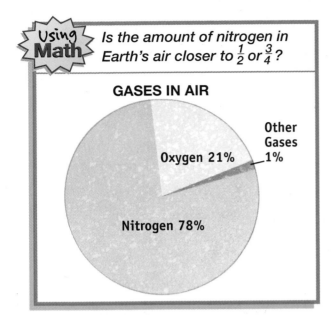

GASES IN AIR

Oxygen 21%

Other Gases 1%

Nitrogen 78%

A Life-Support System

Life on Earth depends on the gases in air. For example, all animals need oxygen from the air to use the energy that is in the food they eat. Plants need carbon dioxide in order to make food. Study the picture below to see how air provides a life-support system for the living things on Earth. Look for one way in which oxygen, which is used by animals, is added to air.

▼ **The gases in air make life possible.**

Carbon dioxide from the air is used by plants to make food.

Water vapor makes clouds, and therefore rain, possible.

Oxygen is given off to the air when plants make food.

Oxygen from the air is used by animals to release energy from food.

Nitrogen from the air is used by bacteria on plant roots. The bacteria change nitrogen into materials that plants use to grow.

Water and nitrogen-containing materials in the soil are used by plants to make food and to grow.

Earth's Blanket of Air

Imagine that you are riding in a space shuttle. You look down and see patterns of clouds in constant motion above Earth. These clouds are part of a blanket of air that surrounds Earth. This blanket of air, made up of gases, liquids, and some solid matter, is called the **atmosphere**. The atmosphere reaches from the ground to about 700 km (435 mi) above Earth's surface.

As you can see in the diagram on the next page, the atmosphere is made up of four main layers. The farther a layer is from Earth's surface, the farther apart are the particles of air in that layer.

Of the four main layers, the one farthest from Earth's surface is the thermosphere (thur′mō sfir). The particles of air in this layer may be as far apart as 10 km (6 mi)!

Only the lowest layer of the atmosphere has enough air to support life. This layer, called the **troposphere** (trō′pō sfir), starts at Earth's surface and goes up about 8 km–16 km (5 mi–10 mi) above the surface. Most of the oxygen, nitrogen, carbon dioxide, and water vapor in the atmosphere is found in this layer.

In the lower part of the troposphere, particles that make up air are packed close together. But you would need a supply of oxygen to help you breathe

Science in Literature

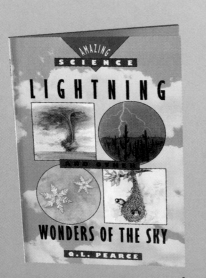

Lightning and Other Wonders of the Sky
by Q. L. Pearce
Illustrated by Mary Ann Fraser
Julian Messner, 1989

A FROGGY DAY

"On June 16, 1882, the people of Dubuque, Iowa, were pelted with hailstones that had tiny frogs trapped inside. These unfortunate animals were probably sucked into the clouds from nearby streams and ponds by strong updrafts, then quickly frozen and covered with layers of ice."

This story comes from *Lightning and Other Wonders of the Sky* by Q. L. Pearce. You will be amazed at what can happen in the world of weather. Read this book to learn about all sorts of weather wonders!

Thermosphere
extends to about 700 km (420 mi) above Earth

Mesosphere
extends to about 80 km (50 mi) above Earth

Stratosphere
extends to about 48 km (30 mi) above Earth

Troposphere
extends to about 16 km (10 mi) above Earth

Height of Mount Everest
8,848 m (29,028 ft)

Height of jetliner
9,000 m (30,000 ft)

Height of Sears Tower
436 m (1,454 ft)

Using Math *How much higher does the mesosphere extend above Earth than does the stratosphere?*

at the top of Mount Everest. The troposphere is the only layer that supports life. This layer is also where weather occurs.

Sometimes a Wet Blanket

What's the weather like today where you live? Is it wet and chilly? Hot and dry? *Hot, wet, cold, dry, cool, warm, windy, chilly, rainy, foggy, sunny,* and *cloudy* are all words used to talk about weather. Those words are actually ways of describing what's happening in the atmosphere.

Weather is the condition of the atmosphere at a certain place and time. It can change from minute to minute. Air temperature and the amount of water vapor in the air greatly affect weather. Without the atmosphere, there would be no weather. What place do you know of where there is no weather? ■

Internet Field Trip
Visit **www.eduplace.com** to explore the atmosphere.

Not Too Warm, Not Too Cold

Reading Focus How is Earth's atmosphere like the glass of a greenhouse?

SCIENCE TECHNOLOGY & SOCIETY

Have you ever visited a gardener's greenhouse? A greenhouse is usually made of glass. The glass lets in sunlight, which warms the ground and other surfaces inside the greenhouse. As these surfaces warm, they release heat into the air. The glass keeps this heat from escaping. This is similar to the way the inside of a car heats up when sunlight shines through closed windows. The air inside the greenhouse stays warm enough for plants to grow throughout the year.

Earth's Greenhouse

In some ways, Earth's atmosphere acts like the glass of a greenhouse. It allows the Sun's rays to pass through it and heat Earth's land and water. Some of the heat from the warmed Earth then goes back into the atmosphere as invisible rays. Some of these heat rays escape into space. But most are trapped by water vapor, carbon dioxide, and other gases of Earth's atmosphere. So the atmosphere warms up.

The gases send some of this heat back toward Earth's surface, as shown

Plants are grown in a greenhouse like this one. ▼

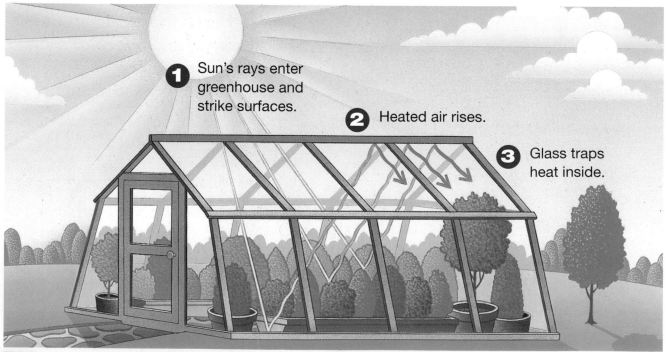

1 Sun's rays enter greenhouse and strike surfaces.

2 Heated air rises.

3 Glass traps heat inside.

in the diagram below. So the air in the lower atmosphere stays warm enough for life to exist. This process in which heat from Earth is trapped by the atmosphere is called the **greenhouse effect**.

Without the greenhouse effect, Earth would be a much colder place. For example, the Moon has no atmosphere. Without an atmosphere, there is no greenhouse effect. So the Moon's surface gets much colder than any place on Earth, as low as $-173°C$ $(-279°F)$. The atmosphere keeps Earth's average surface temperature at about $14°C$ $(57°F)$.

The amount of carbon dioxide in the air is increasing. Because of this fact, some scientists think that the greenhouse effect may be increasing, raising Earth's average surface temperature. ■

The greenhouse effect on Earth ▼

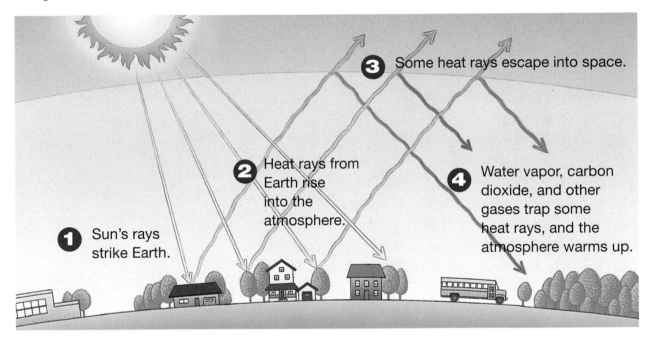

3 Some heat rays escape into space.

2 Heat rays from Earth rise into the atmosphere.

1 Sun's rays strike Earth.

4 Water vapor, carbon dioxide, and other gases trap some heat rays, and the atmosphere warms up.

INVESTIGATION 1 WRAP-UP

REVIEW

1. What is air made of?

2. Which gas makes up about 78% of air?

CRITICAL THINKING

3. Give evidence to show one way in which the atmosphere is like other matter.

4. Could there be life on Earth without the greenhouse effect? What might happen if Earth lost its atmosphere?

WHY DOES AIR MOVE?

Imagine that it's summertime in a big city. The air feels hot and still. What would the air feel like by the seashore or near a large lake? It's likely there would be a nice cool breeze. Why? Find out in Investigation 2 what makes the air move.

Activity

Warming the Air

What happens when the Sun's rays strike your body? Some of the light energy changes to heat and warms your body. Earth's surface is warmed by the Sun, too. Does this heating of Earth's surface change the air above it? Find out!

Procedure

1. Wrap a cardboard tube in a piece of aluminum foil. Do not cover the ends. Attach the tube to a meterstick, using a rubber band, as shown. Push the tube and rubber band along the meterstick until the bottom edge of the tube is at the 10-cm mark on the meterstick. In your *Science Notebook*, **make a chart** like the one shown.

Type of Surface	Temperature (°C)

Step 1

2. Go outdoors to a grassy area. Hold the meterstick with the zero end touching the ground. Have a group member slide a thermometer into the tube. Wait at least three minutes and then **read** the thermometer. **Record** the temperature of the air.

Step 2

3. **Predict** how the temperature of the air over other types of surfaces will vary. Repeat step 2 over three very different surfaces, such as concrete, bare soil, and gravel. **Measure** the air temperature for three minutes each time. **Record** your data.

Analyze and Conclude

1. Make a bar graph of the temperatures you recorded.

 See **SCIENCE** and **MATH TOOLBOX** page H3 if you need to review **Making a Bar Graph.**

2. **Compare** your results in step 3 with your predictions. How did the temperatures you recorded vary? What can you **infer** about the temperature of the surfaces from the temperature of the air above them?

3. Make a **hypothesis** to explain how the air over Earth's surface is affected by the Sun's warming of that surface.

UNIT PROJECT LINK

For this Unit Project you'll make a class weather station and record weather-related data. In the outside area set aside for your weather station, use a rubber band to attach a thermometer to a milk carton. For two weeks, record the temperature in the morning, at noon, and late in the afternoon.

 **Technology Link**

For more help with your Unit Project, go to **www.eduplace.com**.

Activity

Making an Air Scale

Does temperature affect the way air moves? In this activity you'll find out!

Procedure

1. Cut one 20-cm and two 10-cm lengths of string. Tie one end of the long string to the center of a meterstick.

2. Open two large paper bags fully. Turn each bag upside down. Tape one end of a 10-cm string to the center of one bag bottom. Do the same with the other bag. Tape the free end of each string to opposite ends of the meterstick. The open end of each bag should hang toward the floor.

3. On a high table, place a second meterstick between two books in a stack of heavy books. About one third of the meterstick should hang over the edge of the table. Tape the string from the center of the first meterstick to the end of this meterstick. The bags should hang freely and be in balance with one another.

Step 3

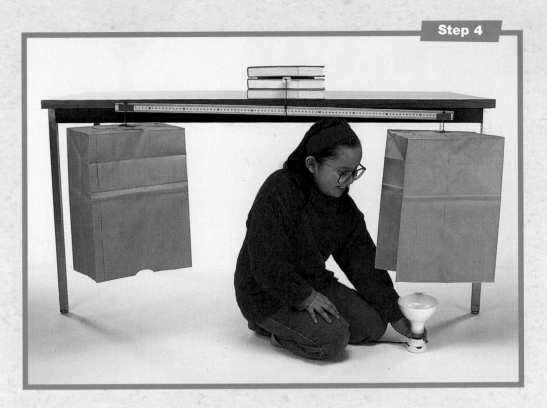

4. Put a lamp below one of the bags, as shown. **Talk with your group** and **predict** what will happen to the bag when the lamp is turned on. **Record** your prediction in your *Science Notebook*. **Measure** and **record** the temperature inside the two bags.

See **SCIENCE** *and* **MATH TOOLBOX** page H8 if you need to review *Using a Thermometer.*

5. Turn on the lamp and **observe** what happens. Again **measure** the temperature inside the two bags. **Record** your data and observations. Let the lamp cool. Then repeat your measurements to check your results.

Analyze and Conclude

1. **Describe** what happened to the bag over the lamp. How does this result **compare** with your prediction?

2. **Compare** the temperature of the air in the two bags in steps 4 and 5. **Infer** the effect of temperature on the weight of the air in each of the bags. Give reasons for the inference you make.

Hot-Air Balloon

Reading Focus What must you do to raise and lower a hot-air balloon?

The hot-air balloon shown below doesn't look like a paper bag, does it? But it *does* work like the paper-bag scale described on pages E18 and E19. Read and find out why.

4 The pilot controls how high the balloon rises. To make the balloon rise higher, the pilot burns more fuel to heat the air more. To lower the balloon the pilot lets the air cool.

3 Heat makes the particles of air inside the balloon move farther apart, so the air gets lighter. Outside the balloon the particles of air are more closely packed together, so this air is heavier. As the warm air rises and fills the balloon, the balloon goes up.

1 The pilot and passengers stand in the basket. The fuel tanks are also inside the basket. Hot-air balloons use propane gas as fuel.

2 A fuel line feeds gas to the burner. The burner hangs above the basket and below the mouth of the balloon. Flames from the burner heat the air in the lower part of the balloon.

mouth

burner

fuel line

basket

Feeling the Air

> **Reading Focus** What causes wind or moving air?

The activity on pages E16 and E17 shows that some surfaces on Earth are warmed more than others. This leads to greater warming of the air over some surfaces than over others.

Moving Air

Look at the photos on this page. They show some of the different materials that make up Earth. In general, dark-colored materials heat up more rapidly than light-colored materials do. So the air above dark-colored surfaces is warmer than the air above light-colored surfaces.

The activity on pages E18 and E19 shows how heating the air in a paper bag makes that bag lighter than an unheated bag. The bag with the heated air moves upward.

When an area of air is warmed, the particles of the warm air spread out. The warm air becomes lighter than the cooler air above it. The warm air rises and the cooler air sinks. The movement of air is called **wind**. Wind is caused by the uneven heating of Earth's surface.

Although you can't see air, you can *feel* it when the wind blows! Wind can be gentle or strong. It can set a leaf softly on the ground or blow down an entire tree.

▲ **Which of these surfaces, do you think, heats up most rapidly?**

Cooler air over land moves out toward the water and takes the place of the rising air.

Warm air over the water rises.

LAND BREEZE

cool land

warm sea

Warm air over the land rises.

Cooler air over the water moves toward land and takes the place of the warmer air that has risen.

SEA BREEZE

warm land

cool sea

▲ The uneven heating of land and water causes land and sea breezes.

Land and Sea Breezes

Let's look at the movement of air between two very different areas on Earth's surface: water and land. Land loses heat faster than water. So at night, the air over land cools off more than does the air over water. Land also heats up faster than water. So during the day, the air over land is heated more than is the air over water. Thus, land and water are heated unevenly.

How does it feel when you walk barefoot on the hot sand at a beach? Your feet may feel as if they are burning. But when you go into the cool water, your feet stop burning. Your body may feel a cool breeze when you come out of the water. Such breezes can make a shoreline a very comfortable place to be in hot weather. Look at the drawings to learn more about what causes land and sea breezes. ■

═══════ **INVESTIGATION 2 WRAP-UP** ═══════

REVIEW

1. Which heats up more rapidly—a dark surface or a light surface?

2. Which loses heat faster—land or water?

CRITICAL THINKING

3. What is the link between the uneven heating of Earth's surface and air movement?

4. Would you expect the temperature near a ceiling to be the same as or different from the temperature near the floor? Explain.

Word Power

Write the letter of the term that best completes each sentence. *Not all terms will be used.*

a. air
b. atmosphere
c. nitrogen
d. oxygen
e. troposphere
f. water vapor
g. weather
h. wind

1. Water that is in the form of a gas is called ____.
2. The gas that makes up the largest part of air is ____.
3. The condition of the atmosphere at a certain place and time is known as ____.
4. The gas that makes up about 21% of air is ____.
5. The blanket of air that surrounds Earth is the ____.
6. The lowest layer of air surrounding Earth is the ____.

Check What You Know

Write the word in each pair that best completes each sentence.

1. Land loses heat (faster, slower) than water does.
2. The layer of air farthest from Earth's surface is the (stratosphere, thermosphere).
3. When air is heated, it (sinks, rises).
4. Weather occurs in the (stratosphere, troposphere).

Problem Solving

1. Why is carbon dioxide important to the survival of life on Earth? Name one other gas in Earth's atmosphere and explain its importance to living things.

2. You're in a spaceship that takes you high above the troposphere. What would the weather be like there? Explain your answer.

Study the drawing. In your own words, explain how a greenhouse works. Then explain how a greenhouse is similar to Earth's atmosphere.

CHAPTER 2

OBSERVING WEATHER

Have you ever noticed that the leaves on trees sometimes flip upside down in the wind? When the leaves turn like this, some people think it's a sign that rain is on the way. What signs do you observe in nature that make you think it's about to rain?

Connecting to Science
CULTURE

Weather Sayings Long ago, people lived closer to nature. Their very lives depended on the weather. Here are some old-fashioned weather sayings from different countries. What weather sayings do you know?

Windy March and rainy April
Bring a flowery and beautiful May.
From Spain

If woolly worms are fat and black
   in late fall,
Expect bad weather.
If they are light brown,
   Expect a mild winter.
From the United States

Red sky at night,
Sailor's delight.
Red sky in morning,
Sailors take warning.
From England

When spiders weave their
   webs by noon,
Fine weather is coming soon.
From Japan

Coming Up

◀ What other weather sayings, rhymes, or songs do you know that tell about the weather?

WHAT IS AIR PRESSURE?

Air pushes down on Earth's surface. Air pushes up and sideways, too. How does the way that air pushes against things affect weather? You'll begin to find out in this investigation.

Activity

It's a Pressing Problem

Air pressure is the push of air against its surroundings. Is air pressure always the same, or can it change? How can you find out?

MATERIALS
- plastic soda bottle with cap (2 L)
- 2 small plastic dish tubs
- hot tap water
- ice water
- timer
- *Science Notebook*

SAFETY //////
Be careful when using hot water. Clean up spills immediately.

Procedure

1. Unscrew the cap of an empty plastic bottle. Wait a few seconds. Tightly screw the cap back on.

2. Fill a plastic dish tub with hot water from the tap. Fill a second plastic dish tub with ice water.

3. **Talk with your group** and **predict** what will happen to the capped bottle when it is put into hot water and then into cold water. **Explain** why you made the prediction you did. **Record** your prediction in your *Science Notebook.*

4. Lower the bottle into the tub of hot water. Hold as much of the bottle as you can below the water level. Keep it there for one minute. Remove the bottle and **record** your observations.

 *See* SCIENCE *and* MATH TOOLBOX *page H12 if you need to review* **Measuring Elapsed Time.**

5. Repeat step 4 with the tub of ice water.

Step 5

Analyze and Conclude

1. **Describe** what happened to the bottle after step 4 and after step 5.

2. **Compare** your results with your prediction. **Talk with other groups** about their results.

3. **Infer** what the results have to do with **air pressure**—the push of air against its surroundings. **Explain** what led you to this inference.

INVESTIGATE FURTHER!

EXPERIMENT

Fill the plastic bottle with hot water. Let the water sit in the bottle for one minute. Hypothesize what will happen if you empty the bottle and then quickly screw the cap back on tightly. Test your hypothesis. Compare your results with those from the activity.

Torricelli's Barometer

Reading Focus What events led to the making of the first barometer?

A **barometer**, a device that measures air pressure, is made in the activity on pages E28 and E29. More than 350 years ago, the very first barometer was made by accident.

A scientist named Evangelista Torricelli (tôr ə chel'ē) was trying to make a vacuum (vak'yo͞om), a space in which there is no air or any other kind of matter. He used a large bowl and a long glass tube that was open at one end and closed at the other.

Torricelli filled the tube with a heavy liquid metal, called mercury, and turned the tube upside down in the bowl. Some mercury flowed out of the tube, leaving a space at the top. The space was the vacuum Torricelli wanted to investigate.

Torricelli wondered why *all* of the mercury didn't flow out of the tube. He also questioned why the height of the mercury changed from day to day. He inferred that air was holding up the mercury in the tube.

As the diagram shows, air pushes down on the surface of the mercury in the bowl. This air pressure keeps some of the mercury inside the tube. And because air pressure keeps changing, the mercury level keeps changing.

◀ **Mercury barometers very similar to Torricelli's are still used today.**

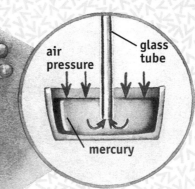

air pressure · glass tube · mercury

All About Pressure

Reading Focus What causes air pressure to differ from place to place?

You live in an atmosphere in which the billions of particles that make up air are in constant motion. These particles move in all directions—up, down, and sideways. When air particles bump into things—a tree, a dog, a pencil, a person, or other air particles—they push. The push of air against its surroundings is called **air pressure**.

You can see the effect of air pressure when you blow up a balloon. When the opening is tied shut, air pushes in all directions at once against the inside of the inflated balloon.

▲ **Blow up a balloon to feel air pressure at work.**

Gravity Rules

Look at the drawing. Are the particles of air closest together near sea level or at the top of the mountain? Do you know why?

Air is matter. Like all matter, particles of air are pulled toward Earth's surface by a force called gravity. The closer you are to sea level, the more particles of air there are squeezed into a given space. Suppose you climbed to the top of the highest mountain, Mount Everest. Three quarters of all the air particles in the atmosphere would be below you.

▼ **The particles of air are closest together near sea level.**

Internet Field Trip

Visit **www.eduplace.com** to learn more about Earth's atmosphere and air pressure.

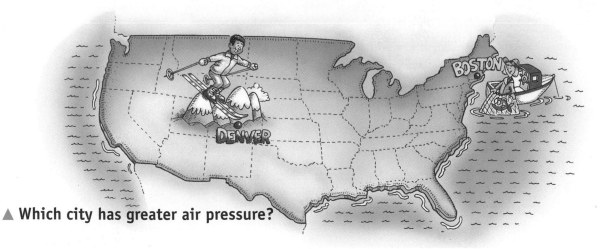

▲ **Which city has greater air pressure?**

Who's Under Pressure?

What difference does it make how many particles of air are squeezed into a given space? A lot! The closer the air particles are to each other, the more pressure the air has.

Denver is called the Mile High City because it is about a mile above sea level. Boston is just above sea level. In which city are people under greater air pressure? If you said Boston, you're right! People who live at sea level are at the "bottom" of Earth's atmosphere. All the air of the atmosphere is above them.

People in Denver are also under pressure. But the higher you go, the less air there is above you. The higher you go, then, the farther apart the particles of air are. So the air pressure in Denver is lower than in Boston.

Measuring Air Pressure

Air pressure is measured with a barometer. There are two main kinds of barometers—mercury barometers and aneroid barometers.

A mercury barometer works like Torricelli's barometer described on page E30. A column of mercury in a tube rises and falls as air pressure changes.

An aneroid barometer is made with a sealed metal can. The can expands or contracts when air pressure changes. This barometer is similar to the one that is made in the activity on pages E28 and E29.

Air pressure is usually measured in inches of mercury. Air pressure varies from place to place. It can also vary in the same place. At sea level when the temperature is 0°C, the height of the column of mercury is 29.92 in. (75.99 cm). This is called

Using Math *Suppose the air pressure, according to this aneroid barometer, is 30.06 in. How much higher is this air pressure than standard air pressure?*

standard air pressure. As air pressure changes, the height of the mercury column changes.

Air Pressure and Temperature

The activity on pages E26 and E27 shows that air pressure in a bottle increases when the air inside is heated. Air pressure in the atmosphere changes with temperature as well. But air pressure in the atmosphere works in the opposite way from air pressure in a closed space, such as a bottle.

When air in the atmosphere is warmed, air pressure gets lower because the particles of air can move away from each other. When air is cooled, air pressure gets higher because particles move closer together.

Areas where pressure is higher than the surrounding air are called **high-pressure areas**. Areas where pressure is lower than the surrounding air are called **low-pressure areas**. The difference in air pressure between such areas can cause winds. ■

Which "block" of air has greater pressure? ▼

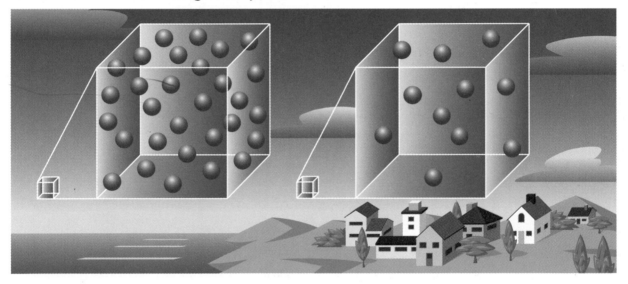

INVESTIGATION 1 WRAP-UP

REVIEW

1. What is air pressure, and how is it measured?

2. Are particles of air in a given space closer together at sea level or at the top of a mountain?

CRITICAL THINKING

3. You carry a barometer with you to the top of a very tall building. You notice that the barometer reading goes down as you ride up to the 107th floor. Explain what happened and why.

4. Explain how pressure would change as the air temperature falls.

HOW CAN YOU FIND WIND SPEED AND DIRECTION?

Look out a window to observe a flag, a tree, or some leaves on the ground. What can these observations tell you about the wind? In Investigation 2 you'll discover even better ways to measure wind speed and find wind direction.

Activity

A Windy Day

Which way is the wind blowing? In this activity you'll build a wind vane to find out!

Procedure

1. Draw a large cross with its center on a hole in the middle of a wooden board. Mark the end of each line of the cross with one of the letters *N, E, S,* and *W* to stand for *north, east, south,* and *west.*

 Math Hint *Each angle of the cross should be 90° in order to form a right angle.*

2. Remove the rubber bulb from a dropper. Carefully push the pointed end of the dropper into the hole in the wooden board.

3. Tape the middle section from a plastic bottle to a wire hanger. Then insert the straightened end of the wire hanger into the dropper.

4. Cut out an arrowhead and arrow tail from cardboard. Attach these to the hanger as shown. You have made a wind vane.

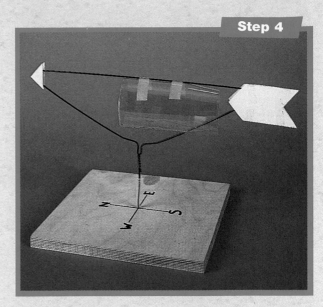

5. Place the wooden board in an open area outdoors. Use a compass to find north. Then turn the wooden board so that *N* is in the direction of north.

6. **Observe** such things as flags and leaves to see how they move in the wind. **Discuss** your observations **with your group** members. **Infer** the direction from which the wind is blowing.

7. A **wind vane** is a device that shows the direction from which the wind is blowing. The arrow of your wind vane will point in the direction from which the wind is blowing. Use the wind vane to **find** the wind direction and **record** it in your *Science Notebook*.

8. **Make a chart** like the one shown. For one week, **observe** and **record** the wind direction. **Record** other weather conditions at the same time.

Date/Time	Wind Direction	Weather Conditions

See **SCIENCE** and **MATH TOOLBOX** page H10 if you need to review *Making a Chart to Organize Data.*

Analyze and Conclude

1. **Compare** your findings in step 7 with the inference you made in step 6.

2. Use the data in your chart to **infer** whether the wind comes from the same direction on warm days as it does on cool days. What connections do you see between the direction of the wind and other weather conditions over a period of time? What patterns do you see? Explain.

Activity

How Fast the Wind Blows

Have you heard a weather reporter talk about the speed of the wind? Perhaps you've wondered how wind speed is measured. In this activity you'll build an anemometer, a device to measure wind speed.

MATERIALS
- goggles
- stapler
- 4 plastic straws
- 4 small paper cups
- tape
- crayon
- straight pin
- pencil with a new eraser
- timer
- *Science Notebook*

SAFETY /////

Wear goggles during this activity. Be careful when handling the straight pin.

Procedure

1. Staple one end of a plastic straw to the outside of a paper cup, near the rim. Do the same thing with three other straws and paper cups. Each straw should be sticking out to the *right* of its cup.

2. Place two cups on their sides with the straws pointed toward each other. The open ends of the cups should be facing in opposite directions. Overlap the tips of the straws about 1 cm and tape them together.

3. Repeat step 2 with the other two cups. Then crisscross the two pairs of straws, as shown. Tape the two pairs of straws together at their midpoints. Mark the bottom of one cup with an *X*.

Step 3

Step 1

4. Your teacher will insert a straight pin through the center of the cross and into the top of a pencil eraser. Don't push the pin all the way in. Your anemometer (an ə mäm'-ət ər) is complete.

5. Test your anemometer by holding the pencil and blowing into the cups. The cups should spin freely. You can watch for the cup marked *X* on the bottom to tell when the anemometer has made one complete spin.

6. Talk with your group members and **hypothesize** how your anemometer can be used to measure wind speed. **Record** and **explain** your hypothesis in your *Science Notebook*.

7. Make a chart like the one shown. Take your anemometer outside. **Count** how many times it spins in one minute. **Record** the number of spins at different times of the day or at the same hour each day for one week. **Record** other observations about weather conditions at the same time.

Date	Time	Spins in 1 min	Weather Conditions

Analyze and Conclude

1. Study the data in your chart. **Compare** differences in wind speed at different times and under different weather conditions. **Describe** any patterns you see.

2. Compare the hypothesis you made in step 6 with your results.

Technology *Link*
CD-ROM

INVESTIGATE FURTHER!

Use the **Science Processor CD-ROM**, *Weather and Climate* (Investigation 2, Windswept) to find out how wind speed is used to assess severe weather conditions.

E37

Which Way Is the Wind Blowing?

Reading Focus How can you find wind direction and wind speed?

Wind is moving air. In Chapter 1 you saw that the uneven heating of Earth results in the uneven heating of air. Recall that differences in air temperature affect air pressure. Winds occur when there are differences in air pressure between two areas of air that are near each other. Winds move from areas of high pressure to areas of low pressure.

Finding Wind Direction

The direction of the wind is the direction from which it is blowing. A wind blowing from the east to the west is called an east wind.

A **wind vane** is a device that shows wind direction. Most wind vanes are shaped like a long arrow with a tail. When the wind blows, the arrow points into the wind. If the arrow points south, the wind is a south wind.

Another instrument used to find wind direction is a windsock. A **windsock** is a cloth bag that is narrow at one end and open at both ends. Air enters the wide end and causes the narrow end to point away from the direction that the wind is blowing. This is opposite to what the wind vane does.

Measuring Wind Speed

What makes some winds stronger than others? The greater the difference in air pressure between two areas, the stronger the winds produced. Also, the closer the areas are, the stronger the winds produced.

▲ A windsock points away from the wind.

A wind vane points into the wind. On this wind vane, the head of the horse points into the wind. ▶

An **anemometer** is a device used to measure wind speed. It often consists of cups on spokes attached to a pole. Scientists use an anemometer like the one shown below to record wind speed in kilometers per hour (km/h). The activity on pages E36 and E37 uses spins per minute to record wind speed.

If you don't have special devices to measure wind speed, you can try to figure out wind speed using the Beaufort (bō'fərt) scale. In 1805 a British naval officer named Sir Francis Beaufort made a scale that divides wind strength into 12 different categories. Part of the Beaufort scale is shown below. ■

THE BEAUFORT SCALE

Beaufort Number	Speed in km/h (mph)	Description	Observations on Land
2	6–11 (4–7)	light breeze	leaves rustle, wind felt on face; wind vanes move
4	20–28 (13–18)	moderate breeze	dust and paper blow; small branches sway
6	39–49 (25–31)	strong breeze	umbrellas hard to open; large branches sway
8	62–74 (39–46)	gale	walking is very difficult; twigs break off trees
10	89–102 (55–63)	whole gale	much damage to buildings; trees uprooted
12	117 and up (72 and up)	hurricane	violent, widespread destruction

◀ **An Optical Broadcasting Wind Indicator measures wind speed and direction.**

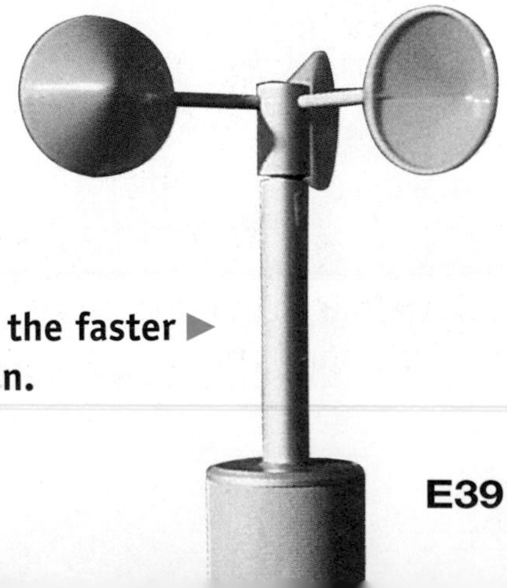

The faster the wind blows, the faster ▶ the anemometer's cups spin.

Wind Power

Reading Focus How can people use wind energy to do work?

SCIENCE TECHNOLOGY & SOCIETY

The activity on pages E36 and E37 shows how to make a device called an anemometer, which measures wind speed. The harder the wind blows, the faster an anemometer will spin. What if all that spinning energy could be put to work?

Early Wind Machines

Windmills are machines that put the wind to work. They were first used in the Middle East, perhaps as long ago as the seventh century. In those early windmills, a wheel made of cloth sails was attached to a tall structure.

As the wind blew, the sails spun. The turning motion was used to grind grain.

In the fourteenth century, the Dutch began using windmills to pump water out of low-lying land. The traditional Dutch windmill has four arms attached to cloth sails or wooden blades. The sails or blades spin like the propeller of a plane. They can turn only when the wind blows directly at them.

▲ Many modern windmills work the same way as this traditional Dutch windmill.

The long curved blades of the modern Darrieus wind turbine can catch wind coming from any direction. ▶

Today's Windmills

Modern windmills are designed to work at much higher wind speeds than are traditional ones. They are usually made of aluminum or other light metals. Some modern windmills, called wind turbines (tur'binz), are used to produce electricity.

The largest wind turbines are over 90 m (300 ft) tall. The blade tips travel as fast as 400 km/h (250 mph). The wind turbine operates a generator that produces the electricity.

Worldwide Use of Wind Energy

Wind power may be one of the answers to today's energy needs. Unlike many other sources of energy, wind can't be used up and it doesn't pollute the air. Also, wind turbines can be built fairly quickly.

But wind power is not a perfect answer to energy needs. The direction and speed of the winds change over

▲ **Wind farm in Altamont Pass, California**

time and from place to place. Sometimes, of course, the wind doesn't blow at all. Wind power works best where wind speeds are high and fairly steady. Wind turbines are placed in areas where there are few trees, houses, or other things that might block the wind.

A wind farm is a system of 50 or more wind turbines working together. Each turbine turns a generator. The Altamont Pass wind farm has over 5,000 turbines. It produces enough electricity to supply several towns in California. Wind farms are being developed in other states as well as in Europe, India, China, and other parts of the world. ■

INVESTIGATION 2 WRAP-UP

REVIEW

1. Name one device used to find wind direction and one device that measures wind speed.

2. In which direction does an east wind blow?

CRITICAL THINKING

3. Most people would agree that wind turbines offer benefits as an energy source for producing electricity. Identify two problems in using wind turbines as a source of energy.

4. Compare how a windsock works with how a wind vane works.

HOW DOES WATER IN THE AIR AFFECT WEATHER?

Water vapor is a very important gas in Earth's atmosphere. In Investigation 3 you'll find out how the amount of water vapor in the air affects weather.

Activity

Make a Rain Gauge

Rainfall is measured with a device called a rain gauge. Make one in this activity.

MATERIALS
- flat wooden stick
- metric ruler
- marker
- aluminum soda can, top removed
- plastic soda bottle (2 L), cut in half
- *Science Notebook*

Procedure

1. Place a flat wooden stick on your desk. Use a metric ruler and a marker to draw a line 3 cm from the lower end. Label this line 1 *cm*. Draw another line on the stick 3 cm above the 1-cm line. Label this second line 2 *cm*. Then draw another line 3 cm above the 2-cm line. Label this third line 3 *cm*.

2. Divide the space between the lower end of the stick and the line labeled 1 *cm* into ten equal parts. Repeat this for each of the other two spaces. Your stick should look like the one shown.

Step 2

Math Hint *Each of the ten equal parts has a measure of $\frac{3}{10}$ cm or 3 mm.*

3. Place an aluminum can, with the top removed, inside the bottom half of a cut plastic soda bottle.

4. Turn the top half of the bottle upside down. Insert the neck of the bottle into the can, as shown. The top half of the bottle will serve as a funnel. You've made a rain gauge (gāj).

5. In your *Science Notebook*, **make a chart** like the one shown.

Date	Amount of Rainfall

6. Put your rain gauge outdoors where it won't be disturbed. Use your chart to **record** the amount of rainfall every day for one month. To **measure** rainfall, put the marked wooden stick along the inside wall of the can. Then empty the can. Be sure to measure rainfall the same way each time. You might want to add your readings and then find the total rainfall for the month. You can use a calculator to help you.

 See **SCIENCE** and **MATH TOOLBOX** page H4 if you need to review **Using a Calculator.**

Analyze and Conclude

1. How would you measure the rainfall if the water overflowed the can?

2. How could you use your rain gauge to measure snowfall?

3. **Talk with your group** and **predict** how the amount of rainfall where you live will vary during different seasons in the coming year. What information will you need in order to make such a prediction?

Step 4

UNIT PROJECT LINK

Choose one of each weather device you have made—barometer, wind vane, anemometer, rain gauge—to put in your class weather station. Explain each choice you made. Use the devices to collect more weather data.

Technology Link

For more help with your Unit Project, go to **www.eduplace.com**.

E43

Snow Around the World

Reading Focus How does snow affect people's lives around the world?

 Over 2,000 years ago, the Chinese scholar Han Ying observed that snowflakes have six points. About 1,700 years passed before people in other places discovered this fact.

You don't have to know about the shape of a snowflake to know how much fun, or how much trouble, snow can be. Take a look at some ways that people around the world deal with "the white stuff."

▲ **UNITED STATES** In 1880 Wilson A. Bentley began photographing snow crystals through a microscope. He took thousands of pictures, but not one snowflake looked exactly like another.

◄ **JAPAN** Sapporo, a city in northern Japan, has long winters with lots of snow. Every February the city holds a week-long snow festival in which groups compete in a snow-statue contest. The sculptures made are very large. Trucks bring in 40,000 tons of extra snow in order to make them.

Using Math *Explain how you could use mental math to find how many pounds of extra snow are brought in for the festival.*

LAPLAND   Cars aren't practical in regions with heavy snowfall. The Saami (sär'mē) are a people who live in the northern parts of Norway, Sweden, Finland, and Russia. Instead of using cars, they train reindeer to pull sleds over the snow. ▶

◀ **THE ALPS**   The northern side of the Alps Mountain range receives about 305 cm (120 in.) of snow a year. People who live there must find ways to avoid avalanches (av'ə lanch əz). An avalanche is a sudden sliding of snow down a mountain. Some avalanches weigh thousands of tons and move at speeds of 160 km/h (100 mph).

THE ARCTIC   The Inuit (in'ᴏᴏ wit) live in the Arctic, which is frozen under snow and ice for as long as nine months a year. To survive, Inuits join together to fish and to hunt. Snow is so much a part of Inuit life that their language has more than two dozen words to describe different kinds of snow. ▶

The Water Cycle

Reading Focus What role does water vapor play in the weather?

Water is not only found in oceans, lakes, and rivers. Water is also found in air as an invisible gas—water vapor. The movement of water into the air as water vapor and back to Earth's surface as rain, snow, or hail is called the **water cycle**, shown below.

The Sun's energy heats bodies of water, causing some water to evaporate into the air. When water **evaporates**, it changes from a liquid to a gas.

As the water vapor in the air cools, it **condenses**, or changes from a gas to liquid water. The water may freeze and become ice or snow depending on the temperature of the air.

Clouds are formed as water vapor in the air condenses. A **cloud** is billions of tiny drops of water that condensed from the air. A cloud that touches Earth's surface is called **fog**. As the drops of water in clouds grow larger, they become heavier. Finally they fall to Earth. Any form of water that falls from the air is called **precipitation** (prē sip ə tā'shən).

Snow, rain, and hail that fall from the air are part of the water cycle. The water that falls to Earth becomes part of the bodies of water on Earth's surface. As the Sun's energy causes evaporation, the water cycle continues.

THE WATER CYCLE

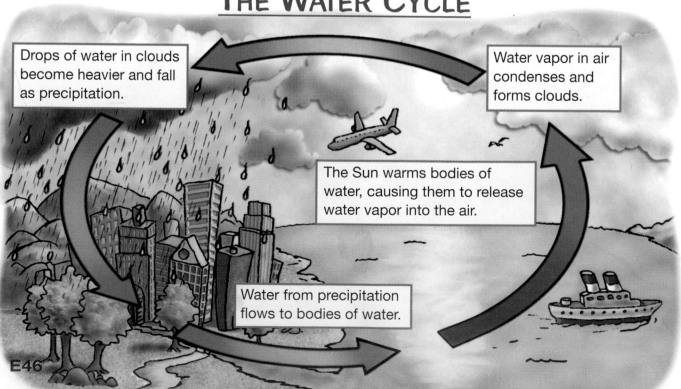

Drops of water in clouds become heavier and fall as precipitation.

Water vapor in air condenses and forms clouds.

The Sun warms bodies of water, causing them to release water vapor into the air.

Water from precipitation flows to bodies of water.

Measuring Precipitation

You've probably heard the amount of rainfall given in weather reports. How do weather forecasters know the amount? They use a rain gauge much like the one made in the activity on pages E42 and E43. A **rain gauge** is a device that measures precipitation.

It's Relative

The amount of water vapor in the air is called **humidity** (hyōō mid′ə tē). There is a limit to the amount of water the air can hold. But that limit can change. The amount depends on the temperature of the air. The warmer the air, the more water vapor it can hold.

The **relative humidity** is the amount of water vapor the air is holding compared to the amount it *could* hold at that temperature. If the air is holding all the water vapor it can at a certain temperature, the relative humidity is 100 percent.

When the temperature outside is high but the humidity is low, the sweat on your skin evaporates quickly. The evaporating sweat carries heat away and you feel cooler.

At the same temperature but with high humidity, the water on your skin can't evaporate quickly. Even though the temperature is the same, you feel warm and uncomfortable.

Science in Literature

Lightning and Other Wonders of the Sky
by Q. L. Pearce
Illustrated by Mary Ann Fraser
Julian Messner, 1989

A FATAL FOG

"In some ways, fog may be the most dangerous of all clouds. If thick enough, fog can prevent you from seeing more than a few feet in front of you . . . . In 1977, thick fog contributed to the worst air disaster in history—two huge passenger jets crashed into each other on a runway in the Canary Islands."

This excerpt comes from *Lightning and Other Wonders of the Sky* by Q. L. Pearce. Fog is just one way clouds can cause disasters. Read the book to learn about a pilot who parachuted from a plane into a thundercloud.

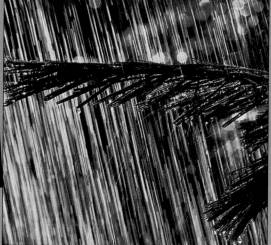

Rain is water drops that are larger and fall faster than drizzle. ▼

▲ Drizzle is very fine drops of water smaller than 0.5 mm (0.02 in.) in diameter.

Hail is particles of ice usually ranging from the size of a pea to the size of a golf ball. Some hailstones are even larger. ▼

▲ Snow is a solid form of precipitation made of ice crystals.

INVESTIGATION 3 WRAP-UP

THINK IT WRITE IT

REVIEW

1. Describe the water cycle.

2. What is used to measure precipitation?

CRITICAL THINKING

3. Imagine that it's a cold winter day. You are outside, talking with a friend. Why can you see your breath as you talk?

4. How can the relative humidity increase if the amount of water vapor in the air remains unchanged?

REFLECT & EVALUATE

Word Power

Write the letter of the term that best matches the definition. *Not all terms will be used.*

a. air pressure
b. anemometer
c. barometer
d. humidity
e. precipitation
f. water cycle
g. wind vane

1. Device that shows wind direction
2. Movement of water into the air as vapor and back to Earth's surface as a liquid or solid
3. Device used to measure air pressure
4. Amount of water vapor in the air
5. Water that falls to Earth's surface as snow, rain, or hail

Check What You Know

Write the term in each pair that best completes each sentence.

1. A device that measures wind speed is called (a barometer, an anemometer).
2. When there is a great difference in air pressure between two areas, winds are (slight, strong).
3. Billions of drops of water condensed in the air form a (cloud, lake).
4. As the temperature decreases, the humidity (increases, decreases).

Problem Solving

1. Explain why an aluminum can "sweats" when you take it out of the refrigerator on a hot day.
2. How can you use a wind vane and an anemometer to help you fly a kite?
3. Suppose you want to find wind speed, wind direction, and air pressure. Which instruments would you use? Explain how each instrument works.

BUILD YOUR PORTFOLIO

Study the drawing. It shows air pressure readings in inches of mercury. They were taken in different places at the same time on the same day. Explain in writing why the air pressure readings are different.

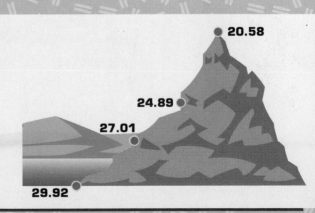

20.58
24.89
27.01
29.92

CHAPTER 3

WEATHER PATTERNS

When you listened to the radio, the weather forecaster said it was going to be sunny for your outdoor field trip. But then it rained all day. In this chapter you'll find out what goes into predicting the next day's weather.

PEOPLE USING SCIENCE

Research Meteorologist You might think that studying weather is not very exciting. But seeing how Anton Seimon learns about storms will change your mind. He flies in a plane above, around, and even into storms.

Anton Seimon is a research meteorologist. He studies storms to better understand how they form and to help other people predict storms. He uses instruments such as thermometers and radar for gathering weather data. He sometimes drops packages of instruments from the plane into a storm that is too strong to fly into. "Studying the information we collect is almost as exciting as flying into a storm," he says.

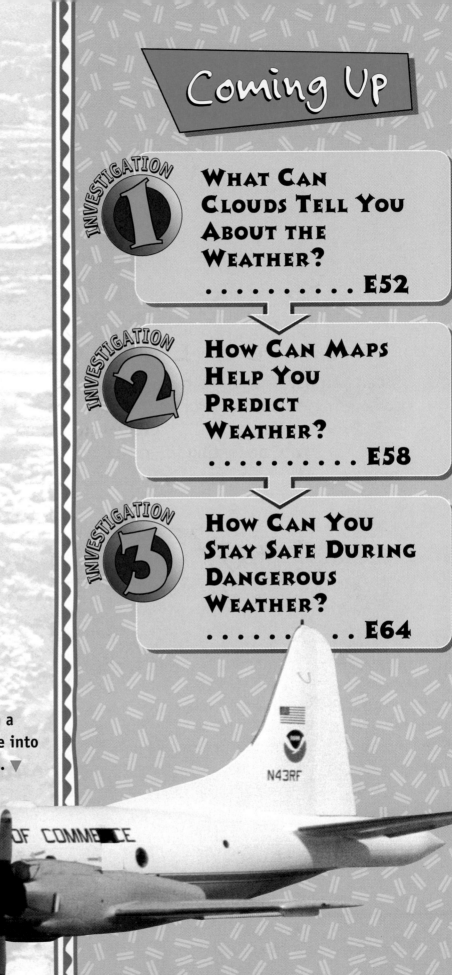

Coming Up

Anton Seimon flies in a plane such as this one into the storms he studies. ▼

N43RF

UNITED STATES DEPT. OF COMMERCE

WHAT CAN CLOUDS TELL YOU ABOUT THE WEATHER?

You're about to head out the door. You notice thin, wispy white clouds high in the sky. Should you take an umbrella or your sunglasses? Find out how clouds can help you predict the weather.

Activity

Kinds of Clouds

Are there different types of clouds in the sky? Discover the answer in this activity.

MATERIALS
• *Science Notebook*

SAFETY
Never look directly at the Sun.

Procedure

Choose three different times of day to carefully **observe** clouds. **Write a description** in your *Science Notebook* of how the clouds look and where they appear in the sky. Then **draw** pictures of the clouds. With your group, **classify** the clouds you saw. Share your results with other groups.

Analyze and Conclude

1. How many different cloud shapes did you see? Did any of the clouds change shape?

2. What colors were the clouds? How high were they in the sky?

3. Explain how your group classified the clouds.

Activity

Cloudy Weather

Can the types of clouds in the sky help you predict what the weather will be? In this activity you'll find out.

MATERIALS
- thermometer
- *Science Notebook*

SAFETY

Be careful when handling glass thermometers. Never look directly at the Sun.

Procedure

1. Think about the types of clouds you've seen in the sky. **Predict** which types of clouds may occur in certain types of weather. **Record** your predictions in your *Science Notebook*.

2. **Make a chart** like the one shown.

Date	Time	Cloud Description	Weather Conditions

3. Twice a day for one week, **observe** the types of clouds you see. **Record** a description of the clouds in your chart.

4. **Record** the weather conditions at the same time you make your cloud observations. Note whether it is sunny, cloudy, rainy, or snowy. Use a thermometer to **measure** the temperature of the air.

Step 4

 See **SCIENCE** and **MATH TOOLBOX** page H8 if you need to review **Using a Thermometer.**

Analyze and Conclude

1. **Compare** your findings with the predictions you made. What might the weather be like tomorrow?

2. **Compare** differences in cloud types at different times and for different weather conditions. **Hypothesize** how clouds might be used to predict the weather.

E53

The Weather From Space

Clouds are one factor scientists use to forecast the weather. **Weather satellites** are devices in space that are used to take pictures of clouds and to collect other weather information. One important type of weather satellite is called GOES, short for the term *Geostationary Operational Environmental Satellite*. This type of satellite travels at the same speed that Earth spins. So a GOES can keep track of weather over the same area day and night.

Weather satellites send images of the clouds over Earth to weather stations on the ground. The satellites also measure moisture in the atmosphere. They provide information about winds as well as the temperature of land and of water. Such data can help farmers know when cold, icy weather is coming. Having this information helps farmers know when they must protect their crops.

GOES can also be used to warn people when big storms are on the way. Weather satellites can track storms over long distances. In 1996, Hurricane Fran was tracked from space for thousands of kilometers over several days.

Using Math *A GOES is shown here with a satellite image of Earth. A GOES orbits at a distance of 36,000 km above a fixed spot on Earth's surface. How many meters is this?*

NOAA
NESDIS
NCDC/SDSD

Watching the Clouds Go By

Reading Focus What are the three main types of clouds, and what type of weather is likely to occur with each?

▲ **Cumulus clouds**

Imagine that you are in a place with no newspapers, radio, or TV. How can you tell what the weather is going to be? Believe it or not, the answer is right outside your window. Just take a look at the sky. The types of clouds that you see can help you predict the coming weather.

But where do clouds come from? Like a magic trick, clouds appear out of the air. That's because they form in air. Look at the diagram to see how a cloud forms.

Cloud Families

As you know, clouds can occur in many different shapes and sizes. The activity on page E52 suggests ways to classify, or group, clouds. In 1803 a scientist named Luke Howard found a way to classify clouds by the way they looked. He classified the clouds into three main families. These families are cumulus (kyo͞o′myo͞o ləs) clouds, stratus (stra′təs) clouds, and cirrus (sir′əs) clouds.

Cumulus clouds are puffy clouds that look like cauliflower. They form when large areas of warm, moist air rise upward from Earth's surface.

Stratus clouds are like flat gray blankets that seem to cover the sky. Stratus clouds form when a flat layer of warm, moist air rises very slowly.

A cloud forms when warm, moist air rises, expands, and cools. ▼

3 Water vapor condenses into tiny drops of water that come together to form a **cloud.**

2 As the warm air rises, it expands and cools.

1 A large area of warm, moist air forms above the ground.

TYPES OF CLOUDS

CIRRUS CLOUDS Often a sign that rainy or snowy weather is on its way

CIRROCUMULUS CLOUDS Thin, high clouds that mean changing weather

CIRROSTRATUS CLOUDS Thin milk-colored sheets that often mean rain is on the way

ALTOCUMULUS CLOUDS Fluffy gray clouds that can grow into rain clouds

ALTOSTRATUS CLOUDS Mean that stormy weather is coming soon

CUMULONIMBUS CLOUDS Thunderheads that bring thunderstorms with rain, snow, or hail

CUMULUS CLOUDS Appear in sunny summer skies

STRATOCUMULUS CLOUDS Mean that drier weather is on the way

STRATUS CLOUDS Low clouds that often bring drizzle

NIMBOSTRATUS CLOUDS Thick dark blankets that may bring snow or rain

▲ Stratus clouds

▲ Cirrus clouds

Cirrus clouds look like commas or wisps of hair high in the sky. Cirrus clouds form when the air rises high enough for ice crystals to form.

Sometimes scientists talk about nimbostratus or cumulonimbus clouds. *Nimbus* is a Latin word that means "rain." When you see *nimbus* or *nimbo-* in a cloud name, you know the cloud is a rain cloud.

Clouds are also grouped by height above the ground. Some clouds are close to the ground, some are high in the sky, and some are in between. Clouds that form high in the sky have the prefix *cirro-* in front of their family name. Clouds that form at a medium height have the prefix *alto-* in front of their family name.

Weather Clues From Clouds

The activity on page E53 explains how to use types of clouds to help predict the weather. You may have noticed that certain types of clouds appear in the sky before a rainstorm. Or you may have seen that other types of clouds show up before fair weather.

Different types of clouds give clues about the weather to come. Examine the different cloud types that are shown on page E56. Which cloud types might tell that rain is coming? Which might tell that the weather will be changing soon? ■

Internet Field Trip
Visit **www.eduplace.com** to learn more about cloud types.

INVESTIGATION 1 WRAP-UP

THINK IT
WRITE IT

REVIEW

1. What are the three families of clouds?

2. How does a cloud form?

CRITICAL THINKING

3. You are going to a picnic when you notice that the sky is filled with a layer of gray clouds. Should you go to the picnic, or should you stay inside? Explain.

4. How can clouds seen from the ground help people predict the weather? What kinds of information do weather satellites provide?

INVESTIGATION 2

HOW CAN MAPS HELP YOU PREDICT WEATHER?

You've probably used maps to find cities and streets. But you can also use a map to find out about weather. Investigation 2 will show you how.

Activity

Weather Maps

How can a weather map be used to predict the weather? Find out in this activity.

Procedure

1. Look on weather map 1 for a high-pressure area, marked with the letter *H*. Find the same high-pressure area on map 2. Note whether the *H* is in the same place or if it has moved. If it has moved, note in what direction it moved. Now repeat this with map 3. In your *Science Notebook*, **describe** what happened to the high-pressure area over the three-day period.

2. Look on the weather maps for a low-pressure area, marked with the letter *L*. Note whether the *L* is in the same place on all three maps or if it has moved. If it has moved, note in what direction it moved. **Record** what happened to the low-pressure area over the three-day period.

MATERIALS
- weather maps
- *Science Notebook*

WEATHER MAP SYMBOLS

▨	Rain
⬚	Snow
Ⓗ	High Pressure
Ⓛ	Low Pressure
▶	Wind Direction
49/32	High and Low Daily Temperatures (°F)
○	Clear Skies
◐	Partly Cloudy
●	Cloudy
▬•▬	Warm Front
▬▲▬	Cold Front

Step 3

3. Look on map 1 for the lines with the little triangles and half circles. These lines show fronts. A **front** is a place where two masses, or areas, of air meet. Cold fronts are shown by the lines with triangles. Warm fronts are shown by the lines with half circles. Find the fronts on maps 2 and 3. Note whether the fronts are always in the same place or if they move. **Record** your observations.

4. **Predict** what weather map 4 will look like. **Draw** a picture of your prediction. Your teacher will give you a copy of weather map 4 so that you can check your prediction.

Analyze and Conclude

1. How do the locations of high-pressure areas, low-pressure areas, and fronts on weather map 4 compare with your prediction?

2. **Hypothesize** how weather maps can help you predict the weather.

UNIT PROJECT LINK

For five days, use the weather devices in your class weather station to measure weather conditions. Use your observations and a weather map to predict the weather each day. Keep track of how often you make the correct prediction. Do your predictions improve over time?

Technology Link

For more help with your Unit Project, go to **www.eduplace.com**.

E59

Weather Wisdom

Reading Focus How have people from different countries used plants and animals to help predict weather?

People have been predicting the weather since long before forecasts appeared on television or in newspapers. But not everyone looks at weather devices such as barometers and thermometers. Instead, some people observe how plants and animals behave. Look at the map below to see some of the signs people have used in different parts of the world to predict the weather.

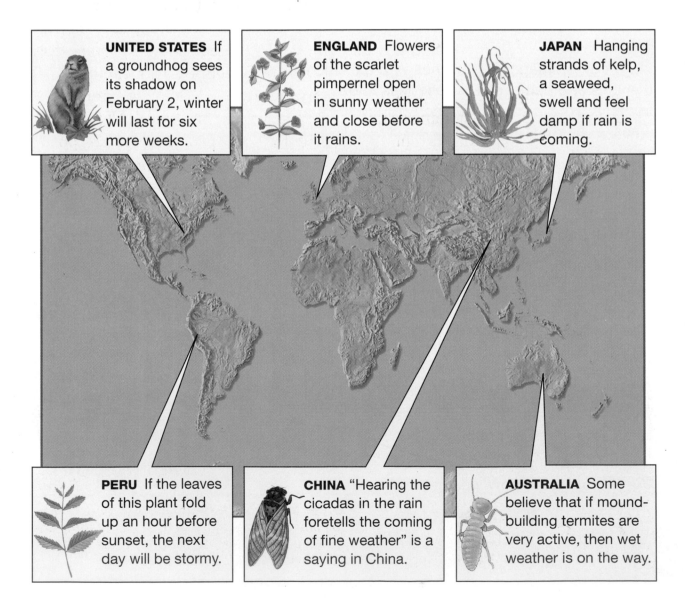

UNITED STATES If a groundhog sees its shadow on February 2, winter will last for six more weeks.

ENGLAND Flowers of the scarlet pimpernel open in sunny weather and close before it rains.

JAPAN Hanging strands of kelp, a seaweed, swell and feel damp if rain is coming.

PERU If the leaves of this plant fold up an hour before sunset, the next day will be stormy.

CHINA "Hearing the cicadas in the rain foretells the coming of fine weather" is a saying in China.

AUSTRALIA Some believe that if mound-building termites are very active, then wet weather is on the way.

Weather in the News

> **Reading Focus** How does a weather forecaster predict the weather?

A **weather forecaster** is someone who makes predictions about the weather. Maybe you've heard a weather forecaster predict bright, sunny skies when, in fact, it rained all day. How do people predict the weather? Why is it such a tough job?

The Weather Detectives

Being a forecaster is a bit like being a detective trying to solve a mystery. First, the forecaster must gather clues, or information, about the current weather. The forecaster gets information from all over the world. The information comes from weather balloons, weather satellites, and weather stations on land and on ships at sea. It tells about such things as wind speed and direction, cloud type, air pressure, temperature, moisture in the air, and precipitation.

Once forecasters have gathered the information, they have to decide what it means. They are like detectives who must sort through the many clues they have uncovered. Fortunately, the forecaster gets to use computers to help solve the "mystery." All the different pieces of information are put into a computer. The computer then puts all the pieces together and produces different types of weather maps, like the ones shown below.

WIND SPEED, M/S

0 2 4 6 8 10 12 14 16 18 20

JPL
Ucla

Using Math *Weather forecasters use computer-generated maps like this wind map (left) and this temperature map (above). In meters per second, what is the greatest speed shown on the wind map?*

Weather Clues

The weather map activity on pages E58 and E59 shows the symbols used for cold fronts and warm fronts and for high- and low-pressure areas. These fronts and areas are clues that a weather forecaster uses to make a prediction. But what do these clues actually mean?

You know that air surrounds Earth. Now imagine that the air is divided into large bodies, or areas. Some of these areas are warm, and other areas are cold. Each different body of air is called an air mass. An **air mass** is a body of air that has the same general temperature and air pressure throughout.

Often different air masses move so that they contact each other. A **front** is a place where two different types of air masses meet. A **cold front** forms

COLD FRONT When a cold air mass meets a warm air mass, the cooler air pushes under the warm air. This forces the warm air mass to rise. Clouds form in the warm air as it is forced upward. ▶

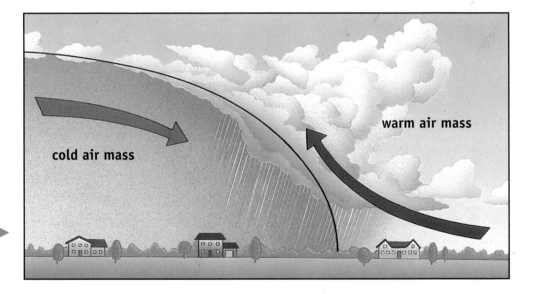

cold air mass

warm air mass

WARM FRONT When a warm air mass moves into a cold air mass, the warmer air rides up over the cooler air. Clouds form as the air rises and cools. ▶

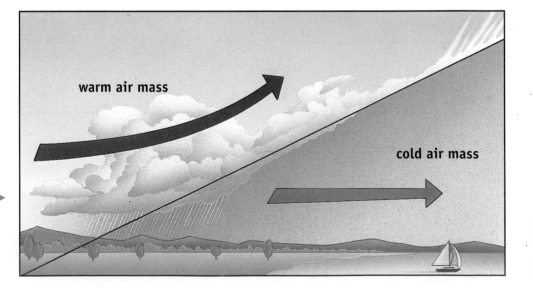

warm air mass

cold air mass

An approaching front darkens the sky ▶ and brings stormy weather.

when a cold air mass moves into a warm air mass. Cold fronts often produce thunderstorms. A **warm front** forms when a warm air mass moves into a cold air mass. Warm fronts often bring light rain.

Weather forecasters also look at air pressure to predict weather changes. In a high-pressure area, or high, the air pressure is higher than in the air surrounding it. High-pressure areas usually bring dry, clear weather.

In a low-pressure area, or low, the air pressure is lower than in the surrounding air. Low-pressure areas usually bring wind, clouds, and rain.

Now the forecaster has enough clues to help solve the mystery. So the forecaster can make a weather prediction. Weather predictions are not always correct. Sometimes weather conditions change so quickly that the information forecasters have isn't up-to-date. And sometimes weather doesn't follow "normal" patterns.

Scientists are developing new ways to gather weather information. These new methods will help forecasters improve their predictions. ■

Technology Link
CD-ROM

INVESTIGATE FURTHER!

Use the **Science Processor CD-ROM**, *Weather and Climate* (Investigation 3, Forecasting) to predict the weather as weather forecasters do.

INVESTIGATION 2 WRAP-UP

REVIEW

1. What kind of weather often occurs at a cold front? at a warm front?

2. What are four types of information that appear on weather maps?

CRITICAL THINKING

3. Suppose you are a weather forecaster for your town. What data would you gather to make a prediction about the next day's weather?

4. Can weather forecasters always be right in their predictions?

HOW CAN YOU STAY SAFE DURING DANGEROUS WEATHER?

The weather may range from calm and quiet to stormy and even dangerous. In Investigation 3 you'll find out about different kinds of dangerous weather and how you can stay safe.

Activity

Storm Safety

In this activity, find out how you can plan ahead and be prepared for severe weather.

MATERIALS
• weather safety reference materials
• *Science Notebook*

Procedure

With your group, make a Weather Safety booklet. In your *Science Notebook,* list the types of severe weather that may occur in your area. These may include thunderstorms, lightning, snowstorms, hurricanes, or tornadoes. Find out which radio and TV stations to listen to in case of severe weather and what safety measures you should take. **Record** what you learn in your Weather Safety booklet.

Analyze and Conclude

1. Where should you go if you are warned that severe weather is about to strike your area?

2. What things should you do or not do during severe weather?

Activity

Tornado Tube

Have you ever seen a tornado? These dangerous twisting storms can cause a lot of damage. If you have never seen a tornado, don't worry. In this activity you'll be making a model of one.

MATERIALS
- 2 plastic soda bottles (2 L)
- water
- tornado tube
- *Science Notebook*

Procedure

1. Fill a plastic soda bottle about two-thirds full of water.

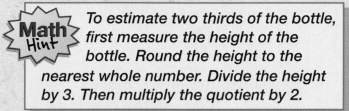

Math Hint *To estimate two thirds of the bottle, first measure the height of the bottle. Round the height to the nearest whole number. Divide the height by 3. Then multiply the quotient by 2.*

2. Screw one end of a tornado tube onto the bottle. Make sure the end fits tightly. Then screw an empty bottle into the other end of the tube. Make sure it also is screwed in tightly.

3. Turn the bottle with the water in it upside down. Hold on to the tornado tube. Quickly move the bottles in five or six circles so that the water inside swirls. **Observe** as the water drains from one bottle into the other. **Record** your observations in your *Science Notebook*.

Step 3

Analyze and Conclude

1. Describe the motion of the water as it moved from one bottle to the other.

2. Hypothesize how the movement of air in a tornado is similar to the movement of air and water in your model.

Light and Sound Show

Reading Focus What causes a thunderstorm?

KABOOM! You hear a sharp crack of thunder. A **thunderstorm** is a storm that produces heavy rain, strong winds, lightning, and thunder. Every year there are about 16 million thunderstorms around the world. These storms occur along cold fronts and in places where the local weather is very hot and humid.

Stormy Weather

Thunderstorms begin to form when warm, moist air rises from Earth's surface. Sometimes strong winds several kilometers above the surface make the air rise even faster and higher than usual, forming cumulonimbus clouds, or thunderheads. A single thunderhead may be several kilometers wide and up to 10 km (6 mi) high.

Swirling winds within the clouds carry water droplets and ice crystals up and down several times. This action causes the droplets and crystals to grow in size. When the raindrops and ice crystals become large enough and heavy enough, rain or hail begins to fall.

Using Math *This time-exposure photo shows a series of lightning flashes. Lightning strikes somewhere on Earth about 100 times every second. How many times does lightning strike each minute?*

Lightning and Thunder

Water and ice particles inside a thunderhead are thrown together by strong winds. This action produces static electricity. The energy from the static electricity is released as a flash of light and heat, called lightning. As a lightning bolt moves through the air, the air around it can become as hot as 30,000°C (54,000°F). This is more than five times as hot as the surface of the Sun!

As a lightning bolt flashes, it heats the air in its path. The air expands very rapidly, causing the rumbling we call thunder.

Although you might not think so, lightning and thunder happen at the same time. But we see lightning before we hear thunder, because light travels faster than sound.

Thunderstorm Problems

Although thunderstorms cool the air and ground, they can also cause problems. Sometimes there is so much rain from a sudden thunderstorm that floods occur. Sudden and violent floods are called **flash floods**. Heavy rain or hail from thunderstorms can damage crops and destroy property.

Lightning can injure and even kill people. It can cause fires. It can damage power lines and stop the flow of electricity. It can also interfere with radio and TV signals. ■

Science in Literature

MAKING RAIN TO ORDER

Professor Fergus Fahrenheit and His Wonderful Weather Machine
by Candace Groth-Fleming
Illustrated by Don Weller
Simon & Schuster, 1994

"'Good afternoon, ladies and gentlemen,' the stranger said . . . . 'My name is Professor Fergus Fahrenheit, and I represent the Wonder-Worker Weather Company. I understand you folks are in need of some rain. Well, ours is of the very best quality; and with every order we throw in a free silk umbrella.'"

This speech starts the action in *Professor Fergus Fahrenheit and His Wonderful Weather Machine* by Candace Groth-Fleming. Find out how the professor tries to help a town get rain.

Staying Safe in a Storm

Reading Focus How can you stay safe during severe weather?

In the past, people weren't able to predict when storms, hurricanes, or tornadoes would occur. But today, with the help of tools like weather satellites, scientists can better predict the weather.

The activity on page E64 explains how to be prepared for severe weather. What kinds of safety precautions would you include for thunderstorms, hurricanes, and tornadoes? Here are some precautions you should follow.

STAYING SAFE DURING A FLASH FLOOD

Flash floods can result from thunderstorms or hurricanes. Here are things you can do to keep yourself safe during a flood.

- Stay away from rivers, streams, creeks, and sewer drains. Water in these bodies can move very quickly.
- Don't try to walk or drive through water if you can't see the ground beneath the water.
- If a flood occurs, move to higher ground as quickly as possible.

STAYING SAFE FROM LIGHTNING

If you are outdoors:

- Go indoors. If you can't, stay away from tall buildings and trees. Lightning usually strikes the tallest objects.
- Avoid metal objects, such as metal baseball bats.
- Stay in a car, with windows up.

If you are indoors:

- Stay away from metal doors and large windows.
- Do not use the telephone.
- Unplug any TV, VCR, or computer.

In the mountains outside Tucson, Arizona, a flash flood turns an arroyo, or dry gully *(left)*, into a dangerous rush of muddy water *(below)*.

STAYING SAFE DURING A HURRICANE

If you are caught in a hurricane, here are some things you can do.

- Get as far away from ocean beaches as possible. The huge waves produced by hurricanes are very dangerous.

- Stay inside in a basement, under a stairwell, or in another sheltered area.

- Stay away from windows. Hurricane winds can break glass, causing injury to people.

- Listen to local TV and radio stations.

STAYING SAFE DURING A TORNADO

If a tornado is sighted in your area, follow these precautions.

- If you are outside, try to stay in a ditch or other low area. This will help protect you from flying objects.

- If you are inside, try to stay in a basement or a storm cellar. If there is no basement or storm cellar, stay in a closet or bathroom.

- Stay away from windows and doors that lead outside. These can be blown apart by the winds of a tornado.

The Fiercest Storms on Earth

Reading Focus How are hurricanes and tornadoes alike, and how are they different?

What are hurricanes and tornadoes? What causes these storms? Why are they known as the fiercest storms on Earth?

Hurricanes—The Largest Storms

Hurricanes have different names in different parts of the world. They are called cyclones in the Indian Ocean and typhoons in the west Pacific Ocean. **Hurricanes** are large, violent storms that form over warm ocean water.

To be called a hurricane, the storm must have winds of at least 117 km/h (70 mph). Some hurricanes have winds of more than 240 km/h (144 mph)! Hurricanes are classified according to strength. The weakest hurricane is a level 1 and the strongest is a level 5. Look back at the Beaufort scale on page E39. How does the Beaufort scale describe hurricanes?

Hurricanes start out as small thunderstorms over an ocean. Several of these storms may join to form a larger storm. This storm grows bigger as it takes in heat and moisture from warm ocean water. As the storm grows, the wind increases. This causes

These satellite photos of Hurricane Andrew show the storm's location as it moved from Florida to Louisiana. The photos were taken over a three-day period in August 1992. ▼

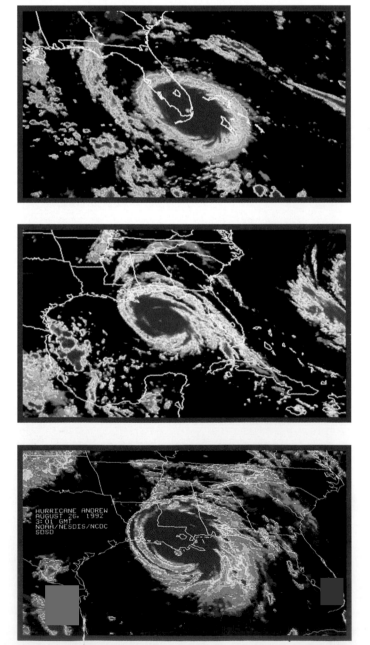

HURRICANE ANDREW
AUGUST 26, 1992
3:01 GMT
NOAA/NESDIS/NCDC
SDSD

the clouds to spin. The diagram on this page explains how a hurricane forms.

In the middle of a hurricane is a hole, called the eye of the hurricane. Within the eye the weather is calm. There is little wind and no rain. Sometimes people are fooled into thinking that a hurricane is over when the eye is overhead. But it isn't over. The other half of the storm is on its way.

Hurricanes are the largest storms on Earth. A hurricane can cover a circular area as wide as 600 km (360 mi). A storm this size could cover both the states of Alabama and Mississippi at one time.

Hurricanes on the Move

Once a hurricane forms, it begins to travel. As it moves, the winds blow harder. The winds can rip up trees, blow off roofs, and produce giant ocean waves. These waves can wash away beaches and sink boats. Rain can cause flooding. Hurricanes don't last long once they reach land. The storm loses its source of energy over land or cold ocean water.

Internet Field Trip

Visit **www.eduplace.com** to find out more about hurricanes and tornadoes.

4 A circular wall of clouds with heavy rains and strong winds develops around the eye. As the warm air moves up, it spreads out.

5 In the eye the air sinks slowly, the winds are light, and there are no clouds.

3 Warm moist air spirals up around the eye.

2 Strong surface winds at the base of the hurricane blow into an area of low pressure.

1 Warm ocean water provides the energy.

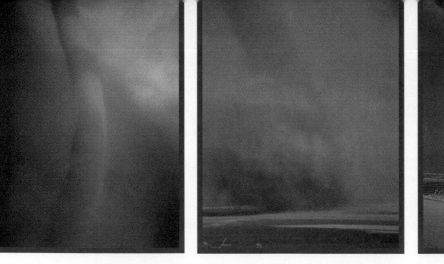

▲ **A tornado may skip across the ground like someone playing leapfrog. Whatever it touches is likely to be destroyed.**

Twister!

Sometimes a thunderstorm produces a tornado. A **tornado**, also known as a twister, is a funnel-shaped storm of spinning wind. The activity that is on page E65 uses water in a bottle to model a tornado. The spinning water is shaped like a tornado. But unlike the water, air in a tornado spins upward.

Tornadoes can develop without warning. They form when a column of warm air begins to spin. As air flows up into this swirling column, it spins very fast, forming the well-known funnel-shaped cloud.

Even though tornadoes don't cover as much area as hurricanes, they can be just as dangerous. The speed of the winds in the center of a tornado can be as high as 500 km/h (300 mph). This is twice the speed of the winds in the worst hurricane!

In tornadoes the air pressure is very low. The strong winds blowing into these low-pressure areas can sweep objects into the tornado, including dirt, trees, and roofs of buildings. The winds may be strong enough to move and destroy large trees, cars, trains, and houses. ∎

INVESTIGATION 3 WRAP-UP

THINK IT WRITE IT

REVIEW

1. Describe the safety precautions you should take if you are outside during a thunderstorm.

2. What causes lightning? Why do you see the flash before you hear the thunder?

CRITICAL THINKING

3. Make a table to compare hurricanes, thunderstorms, and tornadoes. How are they similar? How are they different?

4. What type of dangerous weather is most likely to occur in your region? What precautions should you take if that type of weather occurs?

REFLECT & EVALUATE

Word Power

Write the letter of the term that best matches the definition. *Not all terms will be used.*

a. cirrus clouds
b. cold front
c. cumulus clouds
d. front
e. hurricane
f. stratus clouds
g. tornado
h. warm front

1. Where a cold air mass moves into a warm one
2. High, thin, feathery clouds made up of ice crystals
3. A large violent storm that forms over warm ocean water
4. A place where two masses of air meet
5. A low flat cloud that often brings drizzle
6. A funnel-shaped storm of spinning wind

Check What You Know

Write the term in each pair that best completes each sentence.

1. When a low-pressure area moves into a region, the weather will likely be (rainy, dry).
2. Hurricanes form over (deserts, oceans).
3. The air pressure inside a tornado is very (high, low).
4. Water vapor in the air condenses into tiny drops of water that form a (front, cloud).

Problem Solving

1. Imagine that you can use only two instruments to forecast tomorrow's weather. Which two would you choose? Explain your reasoning.

2. Describe two safety precautions people can take for each of the following types of dangerous weather: thunderstorms, hurricanes, and tornadoes.

Study the drawing. Then write an explanation of how hurricanes form.

CHAPTER 4

SEASONS AND CLIMATE

Do you live in the northern part of the United States? If so, you may go sledding in winter and swimming in summer. If you live in southern California or Florida, you may not have as great a change between seasons. But every place on Earth has seasons.

Connecting to Science
CULTURE

Algonquin Moon The Algonquins, a Native American people, gave a name to each full moon to keep track of the seasons. Crow Moon is the name given to spring because that is when the crows return. April is the month of Sprouting Grass Moon. At the peak of spring is Flower Moon. In June comes Strawberry Moon. The heat of summer begins Thunder Moon, and August is the time of Sturgeon Moon. Summer ends with Harvest Moon. October's moon is the Hunter, and chilly November is the month of Frost Moon. The winter brings Long Nights Moon and then the howling winds of Wolf Moon. By February, food is scarce. That month's moon is named Hunger. How would you name the moon for the seasons where you live?

Coming Up

◀ The Algonquins might call this moon the Long Nights Moon.

WHAT CAUSES THE SEASONS?

Which activities do you like to do in summer? in winter? How do the differences in weather during summer and winter affect what you do? In Investigation 1 you'll find out what causes summer and winter!

Activity

Sunshine Hours

Do the number of hours of sunlight change from season to season? Gather data to find out.

Procedure

1. The table shows the times the Sun rises and sets in the middle of each month. **Interpret the data** in the table to **predict** whether the number of hours of sunlight is greater in winter or in summer. **Discuss** your prediction with your group and then **record** it in your *Science Notebook*.

2. Using graph paper, set up a graph like the one shown on page E77. Note that *Time of Day* should be on the left side and *Month of Year* should be along the bottom. Then **make a line graph** using the data in the table.

MATERIALS
- graph paper
- yellow crayon
- *Science Notebook*

Sunrises and Sunsets (Standard Time) for the Middle of Each Month		
Month	Sunrise (A.M.)	Sunset (P.M.)
Jan.	7:20	5:00
Feb.	6:55	5:34
Mar.	6:11	6:07
Apr.	5:23	6:38
May	4:44	7:09
June	4:31	7:30
July	4:44	7:27
Aug.	5:12	6:56
Sept.	5:41	6:09
Oct.	6:11	5:20
Nov.	6:45	4:44
Dec.	7:15	4:36

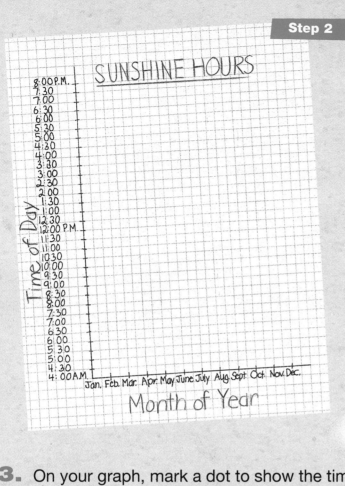

3. On your graph, mark a dot to show the time the Sun rises for each month. Connect the dots.

4. Mark another dot to show the time the Sun sets for each month. Connect these dots.

5. Use a yellow crayon to color the space between the two lines on your graph paper. Keep the graph in your *Science Notebook*.

Analyze and Conclude

1. What does the yellow space on your graph represent?

2. **Interpret your graph**. Are the number of hours of sunlight greater in summer or in winter? **Compare** your results with your prediction.

3. Use the data on your graph to **infer** why the temperature of the air in summer tends to be higher than the temperature of the air in winter.

Changing Seasons

Reading Focus How does the tilt of Earth's axis affect surface temperatures and the seasons?

▲ **How do the changing seasons affect what you do?**

It's the first day of summer! You and your friends are planning a trip to the nearest swimming pool. At the same time, students your age in Australia are spending the first day of winter in school. How can it be summer in one part of the world and winter in another? And why are there different seasons at all?

The Tilting Earth

As Earth moves, or revolves, around the Sun, different places on Earth's surface are heated differently by the Sun. To understand why this

happens, imagine Earth has a line running through it, like the one shown in the picture on page E79. This imaginary line is called Earth's **axis** (ak'sis).

Earth spins, or rotates, around its axis. It takes Earth about 24 hours, or one day and night, to complete this turn.

There is a second imaginary line. It circles the middle of Earth. This line is called the **equator** (ē kwāt'ər). Find the equator in the picture on page E79. The half of Earth that is above the equator is called the

Northern Hemisphere. The half below the equator is called the **Southern Hemisphere**.

When Earth revolves around the Sun, its axis is not straight up and down. Instead, Earth's axis is tilted slightly. The tilt of Earth's axis stays almost the same throughout the year. So as Earth revolves around the Sun, at times the Northern Hemisphere is tilted toward the Sun, and at times it is tilted away from the Sun.

AXIS Earth's axis is an imaginary line that runs from the North Pole through Earth's center to the South Pole.

EQUATOR The equator divides Earth into the Northern Hemisphere and the Southern Hemisphere.

Science in Literature

OUT OF THIS WORLD!

"The Space Shuttle streaks through space at 17,500 miles per hour. It crosses the United States in just a few minutes, and circles the whole planet in just an hour and a half . . . . I could take pictures of giant glaciers in Alaska one minute and of the shallow waters off the Florida coast 15 minutes later."

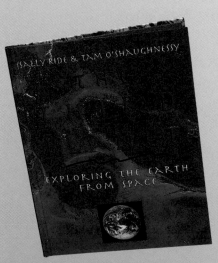

The Third Planet: Exploring the Earth From Space
by Sally Ride and Tam O'Shaughnessy
Crown Publishers, 1994

Here astronaut Sally Ride describes what it's like to look down on Earth from a spacecraft. Her quotation is from the book *The Third Planet*, which she and Tam O'Shaughnessy wrote together. The photographs are out of this world!

E79

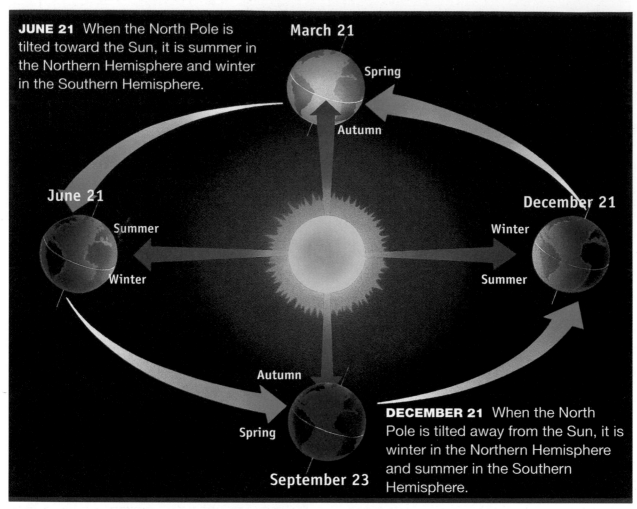

JUNE 21 When the North Pole is tilted toward the Sun, it is summer in the Northern Hemisphere and winter in the Southern Hemisphere.

March 21

Spring

Autumn

June 21

Summer

Winter

December 21

Winter

Summer

DECEMBER 21 When the North Pole is tilted away from the Sun, it is winter in the Northern Hemisphere and summer in the Southern Hemisphere.

Autumn

Spring

September 23

▲ The seasons change as Earth revolves around the Sun.

UNIT PROJECT LINK

Use your weather station to collect data for a two-week period during different seasons of the year. Compare data such as high and low temperatures, amounts of precipitation, and air pressure for each season. Discuss the patterns in seasonal weather you observe.

TechnologyLink

For more help with your Unit Project, go to **www.eduplace.com**.

Seasons in the Sun

Study the picture above. As Earth revolves around the Sun, there are changes in the way the Sun's rays strike Earth's surface. These changes cause the temperature of Earth's surface and atmosphere to change. This leads to the change in seasons.

Remember that the tilt of Earth's axis does not change much. What *does* change is the position of the axis in relation to the Sun's position.

The picture on page E81 shows that, during the winter, sunlight strikes Earth at a slant. When light strikes at

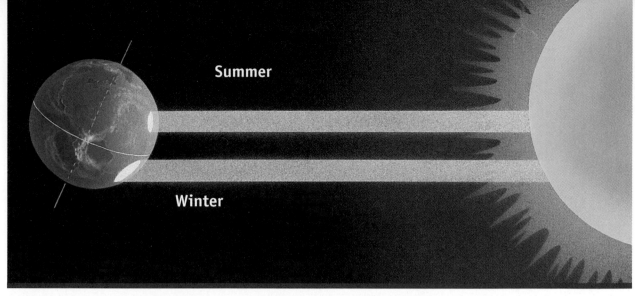

Summer

Winter

▲ The Sun's rays strike Earth at a greater slant during winter.

a slant, it spreads out and covers more area. The greater the slant, the less the ground in this area is heated. This is the main reason that temperatures are colder in winter than in summer.

In summer, sunlight strikes Earth more directly. The light does not spread out as much and covers less area than it does in winter. So the ground is heated more. This is the main reason that temperatures are warmer in summer.

The number of hours of daylight also affects the temperature. When the North Pole is tilted toward the Sun, the Sun appears high in the sky. Then there are more hours of daylight. The longer the Sun shines on an area, the more energy that area can absorb and the warmer the temperatures become.

When the North Pole is tilted away from the Sun, the Sun appears low in the sky. Then there are fewer hours of daylight. Because the Sun has less time to heat an area, temperatures there are cooler. Which season, according to the table in the activity on pages E76 and E77, has the most hours of daylight? ■

INVESTIGATION 1 WRAP-UP

REVIEW

1. Give two reasons why the Sun heats an area more in summer than it does in winter.

2. Make and label a drawing to show the positions of the Northern Hemisphere in summer and in winter. Include the Sun in your picture.

CRITICAL THINKING

3. Suppose the North Pole is tilted toward the Sun. Compare daylight hours at the North Pole and South Pole. Explain your answer.

4. In what season is your birthday? What will the weather likely be on that day in your region? in Australia? Explain your answer.

INVESTIGATION 2

WHAT FACTORS AFFECT CLIMATE?

Climate is the average weather conditions of a place over a long period of time. In Investigation 2 you'll find out what factors cause Earth to have different climates.

Activity

Microclimates Everywhere!

Temperature and wind are important factors in determining climate. Why might two places close to each other have different climates? Investigate to find out.

MATERIALS
- goggles
- cardboard tube
- aluminum foil
- meterstick
- rubber band
- thermometer
- wind vane
- magnetic compass
- *Science Notebook*

SAFETY
Wear goggles when doing step 2. Be careful when handling thermometers.

Procedure

1. In your *Science Notebook*, **make a chart** like the one shown.

Building Side	Temperature (°C)	Wind Direction

2. Cover the outside of a cardboard tube with aluminum foil. Fasten the tube to a meterstick with a rubber band as shown. Move the tube so that the lower edge of the tube is at the 30-cm mark.

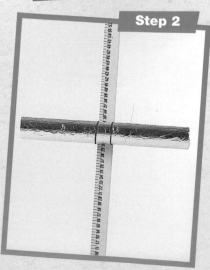

Step 2

3. **Predict** whether temperature and wind direction are the same, or different, on each of the sides of your school building.

4. Take a thermometer and a wind vane outside your school. Stay close to one side of the building and **measure** the temperature 30 cm from the ground. Use a magnetic compass to help **determine** the wind direction, too. **Record** this data in your chart.

 See **SCIENCE** *and* **MATH TOOLBOX** *page H8 if you need to review **Using a Thermometer.***

5. Repeat step 4 for the other sides of the building. **Record** all data in your chart.

Analyze and Conclude

1. **Compare** your prediction in step 3 with your results. What differences, if any, did you find on different sides of your school?

2. Different sides of a building have different microclimates. *Micro-* means "very small." From your study, how would you **define** *microclimate*?

3. Which microclimate was the warmest? Which was the coolest? **Infer** why temperature would vary on different sides of the building.

4. Was the wind direction different on different sides of the building? What factors affect the way the wind blows on one side of your school building?

INVESTIGATE FURTHER!

EXPERIMENT

Predict what would happen if you repeated this experiment over a longer period of time. Would you get the same results? Discuss your predictions with your group. Repeat the experiment once a month for the next three months. How did your predictions compare with your results?

Step 4

E83

Florida Is Not North Dakota

Reading Focus What causes climate and what are three main types of climate?

What is the weather in your area normally like in the summer? What is the weather like in the winter? People in different parts of the world will have different answers to these questions. That's because different places have different climates. The **climate** of an area is the average weather conditions over a long period of time.

Hot or Cold, Wet or Dry

Two important parts of an area's climate are its average temperature and

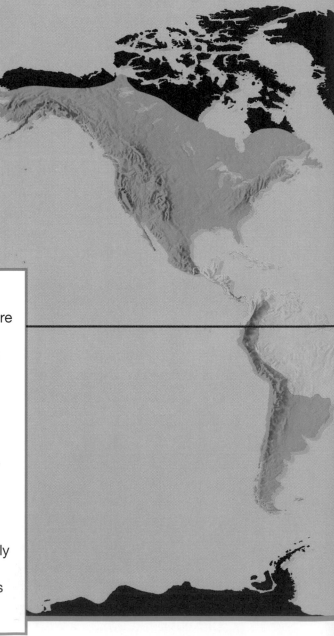

POLAR CLIMATE
In the Arctic and Antarctic, the temperature is usually below freezing. These areas do not receive as much energy from the Sun as other parts of Earth.

TEMPERATE CLIMATE
Between the equator and the poles are areas that generally have warm, dry summers and cold, wet winters.

TROPICAL CLIMATE
The places closest to the equator are usually hot and rainy for most of the year. Temperatures are high because these areas receive the most energy from the Sun.

its average yearly rainfall. The average temperature of an area depends a great deal on how far the area is from the equator. In general, areas close to the equator are warmer than areas farther from the equator. For example, North Dakota is farther from the equator than Florida is, so North Dakota is usually colder than Florida. The map below shows the location of three main types of climates. They are polar, tropical, and temperate.

Areas with a **tropical climate** are usually hot and rainy year-round. Areas with a **temperate climate** generally have summers that are warm and dry and winters that are cold and wet. Areas with a **polar climate** are usually very cold. Which climate do you think you live in?

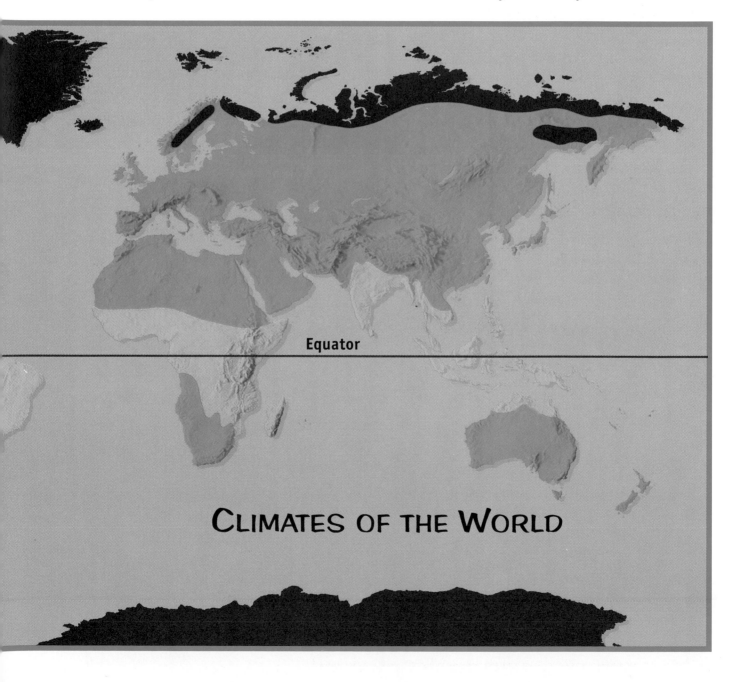

Equator

CLIMATES OF THE WORLD

Air pattern over land near a large body of water ▼

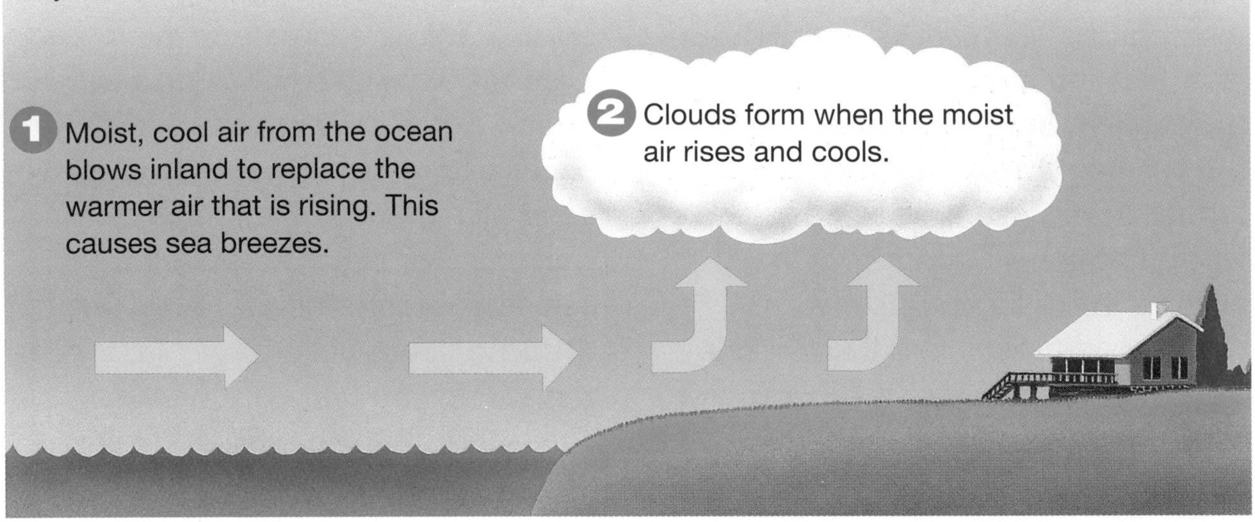

1 Moist, cool air from the ocean blows inland to replace the warmer air that is rising. This causes sea breezes.

2 Clouds form when the moist air rises and cools.

Climate Controls

The activity on pages E82 and E83 shows how to investigate the microclimates around your school building. Factors such as the amount of sunlight and the type of ground cover affect the temperature of an area. Factors such as the placement of buildings and trees affect the way the wind blows in an area.

Just as certain things affect microclimates, certain features, such as oceans and mountains, can affect the climate in an area. In the diagrams on this page and the next, you can see how oceans and mountains affect climate.

If you live near an ocean or large lake, your climate may be cloudier and wetter than the climate of places farther from the water. The summers in your area may be cooler, and the winters may be warmer.

An area in the middle of the plains or far from any large body of water

Air pattern over plains ▼

Plains may be cut off from the sea by mountains. Hot, dry winds blow off the mountains and across the flat land of the plains.

will likely have a different climate. These areas probably will have little rain, hot summers, and cold winters.

If you live near a mountain on the side least protected from the wind, your area may often have strong winds and lots of rain. But if you live near a mountain on the side most protected from the wind, your climate will probably be dry.

El Niño

The cool waters of the Pacific Ocean off the coast of South America become warmer about every four years. This causes weather patterns to change around the world! Scientists refer to this huge area of warm ocean water and the changes in weather patterns that it causes as El Niño.

Severe effects of El Niño occurred in 1997–1998. During the spring of 1998, rainfall was much heavier than normal in the eastern United States. California also had heavy rains and flooding. But, in the southern United States and parts of Asia, drought was the effect of El Niño. El Niño also helped cause forest fires that occurred in Indonesia that year.

Scientists still don't understand all of the factors that produce El Niño. Nor can they accurately predict its effects, but they continue to study El Niño and the weather changes it brings. ■

Air pattern over a mountain ▼

2 These clouds bring heavy rain. As the air passes over the mountaintop and flows down the other side, it becomes warmer and drier.

1 When moist air meets a mountain, the air is forced upward. As the air rises, it cools and forms clouds around the peak.

Clues to Earth's Climate

Reading Focus What are three ways scientists learn about climate changes in Earth's past?

The world's climate has gone through many changes. These changes have lasted from just a few years to thousands of years. Scientists who study Earth's climate look for clues to find out why these changes in climate have taken place.

Tree Rings

One way that scientists learn about climate changes is by studying trees. Most trees grow a new ring every year. You can see the tree rings in the picture. If a ring is wide, the weather affecting that tree was probably moister and warmer than normal that year. That means that the tree probably got plenty of nutrients and grew quickly. If a tree ring is narrow, the weather was probably drier and colder than normal that year. That means that the tree probably didn't get enough nutrients and grew slowly. By studying tree rings, scientists can track warm and cold periods several thousand years into Earth's past.

◄ Tree rings can help scientists determine changes in Earth's climate.

▲ Finding fossils in unexpected places may indicate changes in Earth's climate.

▲ A scientist saws off a piece of an ice core for testing.

Fossil Clues

Another way that scientists learn about climate changes is by studying fossils. Fossils are imprints or remains of animals and plants that lived in the past. Finding fossils in unusual places can be a clue that the climate in an area has changed. For example, some fossilized camel bones were found in the Arctic. Scientists hypothesize that these fossils show that the Arctic was once much warmer than it is now. Fossils can give clues to what Earth's climate was like millions of years ago.

Ice Cores

A third method that scientists use to find out about past climates is to drill holes in glaciers and pull out long columns of ice, or ice cores. Scientists then analyze these ice cores. Finding traces of certain chemicals can give clues about past climate changes. The scientist shown above in the photo on the right is wearing surgical clothing to keep the ice core from getting dirty.

Covered in Ice

Great changes in Earth's climate usually occur very slowly. At times, Earth has been much warmer than it is now. At other times, Earth has been much colder than it is now. Then sheets of ice called glaciers covered large areas of the world. These cold periods are called **ice ages**. The last ice age ended about 10,000 years ago. During that time, glaciers covered much of Earth's land, including large parts of the United States! ■

Technology Link
CD-ROM

INVESTIGATE FURTHER!

Use the **Science Processor CD-ROM**, *Weather & Climate* (Investigation 4, Where on Earth?) to see how the climate in your area is different from those in other places.

Weather Records

Reading Focus What are four kinds of weather records?

GLOBAL views

Have you ever thought that a certain rainstorm was the worst one you'd ever seen? Or, on a hot day, have you ever thought that it couldn't get any hotter? Imagine what it would be like to live someplace that had no rain for 400 years. Think about how it would feel to live someplace that only gets sunlight for half the year. Find out where these places are as you read about some of the windiest, wettest, driest, hottest, and coldest places on Earth!

The Windiest Place
- Winds coming off Commonwealth Bay, Antarctica, can reach 320 km/h (200 mph).

The Fastest Wind Gust
- A wind speed of 415 km/h (250 mph) was recorded on April 12, 1934, on Mount Washington in New Hampshire. This area is known for unpredictable and dangerous weather.

Mount Washington, New Hampshire ▶

STOP
THE AREA AHEAD HAS THE WORST WEATHER IN AMERICA. MANY HAVE DIED THERE FROM EXPOSURE, EVEN IN THE SUMMER. TURN BACK NOW IF THE WEATHER IS BAD.
WHITE MOUNTAIN NATIONAL FOREST

The Coldest Place
- Polus Nedostuphosti (Pole of Cold), Antarctica, has an average temperature of −58°C (−72°F). This area near the South Pole gets sunlight for only about half the year.

The Lowest Temperatures
- The lowest recorded temperature on Earth was −88°C (−127°F) in Vostok, Antarctica, on July 22, 1983.
- In the United States a low temperature of −62°C (−80°F) was recorded on January 23, 1971, in Prospect Creek, Alaska.

South Pole, Antarctica ▶

The Hottest Place
- Dallol, Ethiopia, has an average temperature of 34°C (94°F). Dallol is very close to the equator and is shielded from the Indian Ocean by mountains.

The Highest Temperatures
- The highest temperature recorded on Earth was in Al-Aziziyah, Libya, where the temperature reached 58°C (136°F) on September 13, 1922.
- The highest temperature recorded in the United States was 57°C (134°F) on July 10, 1913, in Death Valley, California.

◀ **Death Valley, California**

The Wettest Places

- Mawsynram, in India, has about 1,186 cm (474 in.) of rainfall per year.
- The state of Louisiana averages 142 cm (56 in.) of rainfall per year.

  In these areas the warm, wet winds blow in off the water. As the winds blow over the land, the air rises and cools. This creates thick clouds and heavy rains.

The Greatest Rainfall

- In one day, from March 15 through March 16, 1952, nearly 187 cm (74 in.) of rain fell in Cilaos, on the island of Réunion, in the Indian Ocean.

▼ Mawsynram, India

The Atacama Desert, Chile ▲

The Driest Places

- Arica, Chile, averages less than 0.01 cm (0.004 in.) of rainfall per year. Chile is near very cold water, so the winds blowing toward land are usually dry and don't form many clouds.
- In the state of Nevada, about 23 cm (9 in.) of rain falls per year. Much of Nevada is sheltered from ocean winds by the Sierra Nevada, a mountain range. The winds that come down from the mountains contain little water vapor.

The Longest Dry Spell

- Desierto de Atacama (the Atacama Desert) in Chile had almost no rain for 400 years! This dry spell ended in 1971.

INVESTIGATION 2 WRAP-UP

REVIEW **1.** What are the two main factors that affect the climate of an area? Discuss each type of climate.

2. How are tree rings clues to climate changes?

CRITICAL THINKING **3.** What would you conclude if you found the fossilized bones of an Arctic animal near the equator?

4. Suppose your business is landscaping. How can you use your knowledge of microclimates?

REFLECT & EVALUATE

Word Power

Write the letter of the term that best matches the definition. *Not all terms will be used.*

1. Climate of places in the Arctic and Antarctic
2. Climate of places closest to the equator
3. Climate with warm, dry summers and cold, wet winters
4. An imaginary line running around the middle of Earth
5. An imaginary straight line running through Earth from the North Pole to the South Pole.

a. axis
b. equator
c. ice ages
d. polar climate
e. temperate climate
f. tropical climate

Check What You Know

Write the term in each pair that best completes each sentence.

1. The greater the slant of the Sun's rays striking Earth, the (more, less) the Earth's surface is heated.
2. A very wide tree ring is likely to form in a year with (much, little) rainfall.
3. The average weather conditions in an area over a long period of time is its (weather, climate).
4. If you live in a tropical climate, the weather is hot and (wet, dry).

Problem Solving

1. You and a friend live in different cities. The cities are the same distance from the equator, but they have very different climates. What are some of the factors that might explain this difference?

2. Your cousin is packing shorts and bathing suits for his trip to Sydney, Australia, on July 3. During his two-week stay, he expects to spend time enjoying warm beaches. What advice would you give him about his trip? Explain.

Study the drawing. Explain in writing how the tilt of Earth's axis and the slant of the Sun's rays cause the seasons.

Using READING SKILLS

Detecting the Sequence

Sequence is the order in which things happen. Sometimes a paragraph contains signal words such as *first*, *then*, *next*, and *later*. When a passage doesn't contain signal words, look for other clues, such as numbers in the text or numbered steps in a diagram.

Look for these clues to detect the sequence.

- Signal words: *first, then, next, later*
- Numbers in the text
- Numbered steps in a drawing

Read the following paragraph. Then complete the exercises that follow.

Earth's Greenhouse

In some ways, Earth's atmosphere acts like the glass of a greenhouse. It allows the Sun's rays to pass through it and heat Earth's land and water. Some of the heat from the warmed Earth then goes back into the atmosphere as invisible rays. Some of these heat rays escape into space. But most are trapped by water vapor, carbon dioxide, and other gases of Earth's atmosphere. So the atmosphere warms up.

1. **Which statement tells what happens first, after the Sun's rays pass through Earth's atmosphere? Write the letter of that statement.**

    a. It heats Earth's land and water.

    b. Some of the heat from Earth goes into the atmosphere.

    c. Some heat is trapped by water vapor.

    d. Heat rays escape into space.

2. **What clues helped you keep track of the sequence?**

Line Graph

This line graph shows the change in temperature during a 12-hour period at Logan Airport in Boston, Massachusetts.

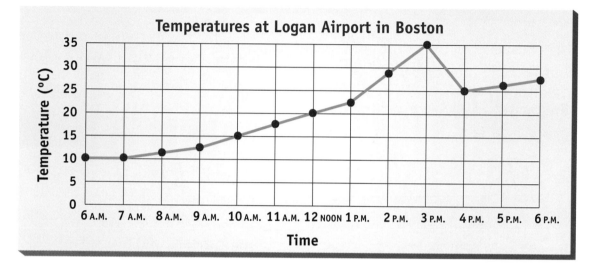

Use the data in the graph to complete the exercises that follow.

1. How many degrees did the temperature change between 6 A.M. and 3 P.M.?

2. What was the difference in temperature between 3 P.M. and 6 P.M.?

3. What was the highest temperature recorded? At what time did that temperature occur?

4. The temperature cooled during a brief thunderstorm in the 12-hour period. Between what hours did the storm take place? How do you know?

5. Make a line graph that shows the data in the table.

Average Monthly Rainfall for New Orleans											
Month	Jan.	Feb.	Mar.	Apr.	May	June	July	Aug.	Sept.	Oct.	Nov.	Dec.
Rainfall (mm)	100	225	100	425	100	200	75	150	150	100	100	200

WRAP-UP!

On your own, use scientific methods to investigate a question about weather.

THINK LIKE A SCIENTIST

Ask a Question

Pose a question about weather that you would like to investigate. For example, ask, "How does wind affect air temperature in a location?"

Make a Hypothesis

Suggest a hypothesis, or possible answer to the question. One hypothesis is that wind will lower air temperature in a location.

Plan and Do a Test

Plan a controlled experiment to find the effect wind has on the air temperature in a location. You could start with two pans holding equal amounts of the same kind of soil, a desk fan, and two thermometers. Develop a procedure that uses these materials to test the hypothesis. With permission, carry out your experiment. Follow the safety guidelines on pages S14–S15.

Record and Analyze

Observe carefully and record your data accurately. Make repeated observations.

Draw Conclusions

Look for evidence to support the hypothesis or to show that it is false. Draw conclusions about the hypothesis. Repeat the experiment to verify the results.

WRITING IN SCIENCE
Letter of Request

Write a letter or an e-mail to ask the National Weather Service for a list of materials they offer to students. When you receive the list, write a letter requesting the items you want. Use these guidelines to write your letters of request.

- Include the parts of a business letter.
- Explain clearly what you are requesting.

SCIENCE and MATH TOOLBOX

Using a Hand Lens

A hand lens is a tool that magnifies objects, or makes objects appear larger. This makes it possible for you to see details of an object that would be hard to see without the hand lens.

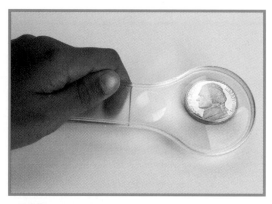

▲ Place the lens above the object.

▲ Move the lens slowly toward you.

Look at a Coin or a Stamp

1. Place an object such as a coin or a stamp on a table or other flat surface.

2. Hold the hand lens just above the object. As you look through the lens, slowly move the lens away from the object. Notice that the object appears to get larger.

3. Keep moving the lens until the object begins to look a little blurry. Then move the hand lens a little closer to the object until the object is once again in sharp focus.

If the object starts to look blurry, move the lens toward the object. ▶

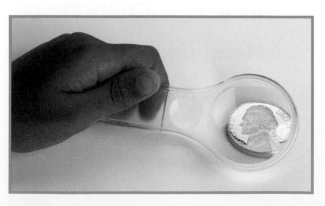

Making a Bar Graph

A bar graph helps you organize and compare data.

Make a Bar Graph of Animal Heights

Animals come in all different shapes and sizes. You can use the information in the table to make a bar graph of animal heights.

Heights of Animals	
Animal	**Height (cm)**
Bear	240
Elephant	315
Cow	150
Giraffe	570
Camel	210
Horse	165

1. Draw the side and the bottom of the graph. Label the side of the graph as shown. The numbers will show the height of the animals in centimeters.

3. Choose a title for your graph. Your title should describe the subject of the graph.

2. Label the bottom of the graph. Write the names of the animals at the bottom so that there is room to draw the bars.

4. Draw bars to show the height of each animal. Some heights are between two numbers.

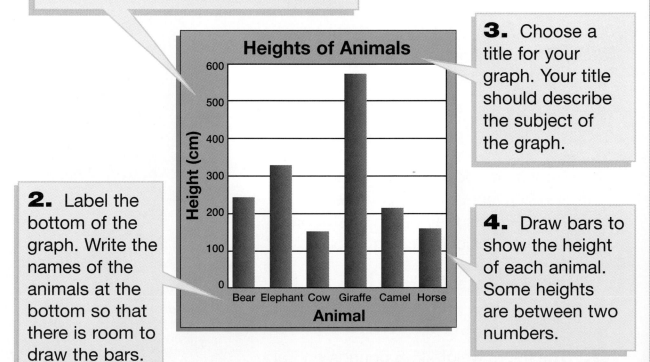

Using a Calculator

After you've made measurements, a calculator can help you analyze your data.

Add and Multiply Decimals

Suppose you're an astronaut. You may take 8 pounds of Moon rocks back to Earth. The table shows the weights of the rocks. Can you take them all? Use a calculator to find out.

Weight of Moon Rocks	
Moon Rock	**Weight of Rock on Moon (lb)**
Rock 1	1.7
Rock 2	1.8
Rock 3	2.6
Rock 4	1.5

1. To add, press:

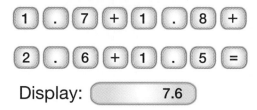

Display: (7.6)

2. If you make a mistake, press the clear entry key (CE/C) once. Enter the number again. Then continue adding. (Note: If you press CE/C twice, it will clear all.)

3. Your total is 7.6 pounds. You can take the four Moon rocks back to Earth.

4. How much do the Moon rocks weigh on Earth? Objects weigh six times as much on Earth as they do on the Moon. You can use a calculator to multiply.

Press:

Display: (45.6)

5. The rocks weigh 45.6 pounds on Earth.

clear entry

divide
multiply

plus
equal

Finding an Average

An average is a way to describe a group of numbers. For example, after you have made a series of measurements, you can find the average. This can help you analyze your data.

Rainfall	
Month	**Rain (mm)**
Jan.	102
Feb.	75
Mar.	46
Apr.	126
May	51
June	32

Add and Divide to Find the Average

The table shows the amount of rain that fell each month for the first six months of the year. What was the average rainfall per month?

1. Add the numbers in the list.

$$
\begin{array}{r}
102 \\
75 \\
46 \\
126 \\
51 \\
+\ 32 \\
\hline
432
\end{array}
$$
6 addends

2. Divide the sum (432) by the number of addends (6).

$$
\begin{array}{r}
72 \\
6\overline{)432} \\
-42 \\
\hline
12 \\
-12 \\
\hline
0
\end{array}
$$

3. The average rainfall per month for the first six months was 72 mm of rain.

Using a Tape Measure or Ruler

Tape measures and rulers are tools for measuring the length of objects and distances. Scientists most often use units such as meters, centimeters, and millimeters when making length measurements.

Use a Tape Measure

1. Measure the distance around a jar. Wrap the tape around the jar.

2. Find the line where the tape begins to wrap over itself.

3. Record the distance around the jar to the nearest centimeter.

Use a Metric Ruler

1. Measure the length of your shoe. Place the ruler or the meterstick on the floor. Line up the end of the ruler with the heel of your shoe.

2. Notice where the other end of your shoe lines up with the ruler.

3. Look at the scale on the ruler. Record the length of your shoe to the nearest centimeter and to the nearest millimeter.

Measuring Volume

A graduated cylinder, a measuring cup, and a beaker are used to measure volume. Volume is the amount of space something takes up. Most of the containers that scientists use to measure volume have a scale marked in milliliters (mL).

Measure the Volume of a Liquid

1. Measure the volume of juice. Pour some juice into a measuring container.

2. Move your head so that your eyes are level with the top of the juice. Read the scale line that is closest to the surface of the juice. If the surface of the juice is curved up on the sides, look at the lowest point of the curve.

3. Read the measurement on the scale. You can estimate the value between two lines on the scale.

This beaker has marks for each 25 mL. ▶

This graduated cylinder has marks for every 1 mL. ▶

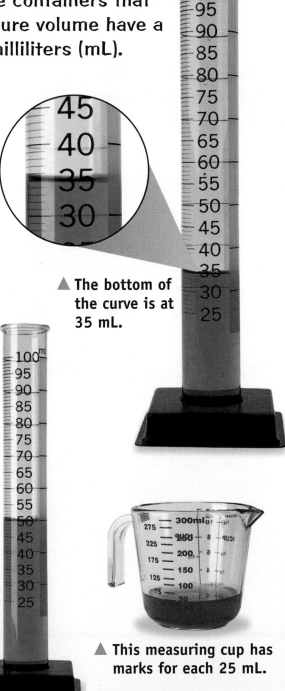

▲ The bottom of the curve is at 35 mL.

▲ This measuring cup has marks for each 25 mL.

Using a
Thermometer

A thermometer is used to measure temperature. When the liquid in the tube of a thermometer gets warmer, it expands and moves farther up the tube. Different scales can be used to measure temperature, but scientists usually use the Celsius scale.

Measure the Temperature of a Cold Liquid

1. Take a chilled liquid out of the refrigerator. Half fill a cup with the liquid.

2. Hold the thermometer so that the bulb is in the center of the liquid. Be sure that there are no bright lights or direct sunlight shining on the bulb.

3. Wait a few minutes until you see the liquid in the tube of the thermometer stop moving. Read the scale line that is closest to the top of the liquid in the tube. The thermometer shown reads 21°C (about 70°F).

Using a
Balance

A balance is used to measure mass. Mass is the amount of matter in an object. To find the mass of an object, place it in the left pan of the balance. Place standard masses in the right pan.

Measure the Mass of a Ball

1. Check that the empty pans are balanced, or level with each other. When balanced, the pointer on the base should be at the middle mark. If it needs to be adjusted, move the slider on the back of the balance a little to the left or right.

2. Place a ball on the left pan. Then add standard masses, one at a time, to the right pan. When the pointer is at the middle mark again, each pan holds the same amount of matter and has the same mass.

3. Add the numbers marked on the masses in the pan. The total is the mass of the ball in grams.

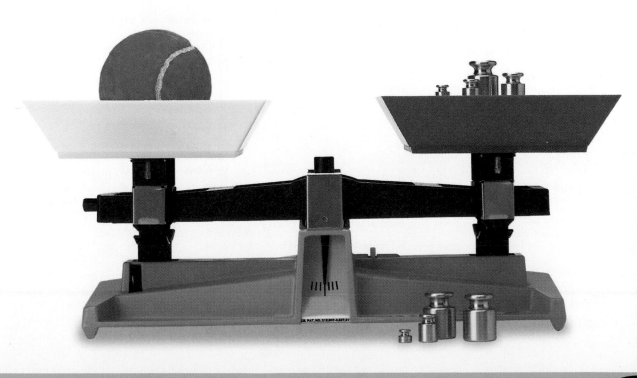

Making a Chart to Organize Data

A chart can help you keep track of information. When you organize information, or data, it is easier to read, compare, or classify it.

Classifying Animals

Suppose you are studying characteristics of different animals. You want to organize the data that you collect.

Look at the data below. To put this data in a chart, you could base the chart on the two characteristics listed—the number of wings and the number of legs.

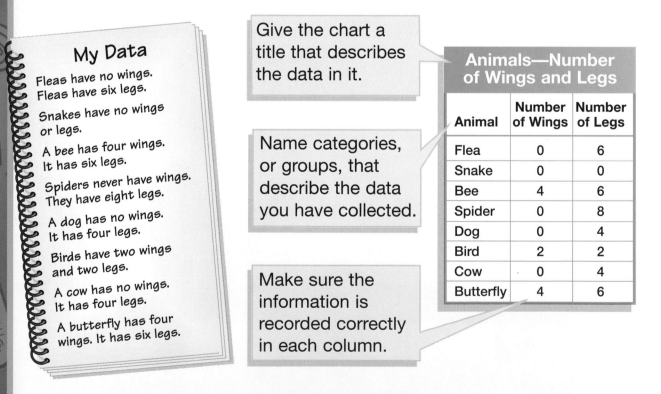

My Data

Fleas have no wings. Fleas have six legs.

Snakes have no wings or legs.

A bee has four wings. It has six legs.

Spiders never have wings. They have eight legs.

A dog has no wings. It has four legs.

Birds have two wings and two legs.

A cow has no wings. It has four legs.

A butterfly has four wings. It has six legs.

Give the chart a title that describes the data in it.

Name categories, or groups, that describe the data you have collected.

Make sure the information is recorded correctly in each column.

Animals—Number of Wings and Legs

Animal	Number of Wings	Number of Legs
Flea	0	6
Snake	0	0
Bee	4	6
Spider	0	8
Dog	0	4
Bird	2	2
Cow	0	4
Butterfly	4	6

Next, you could make another chart to show animal classification based on number of legs only.

Reading a Circle Graph

A circle graph shows a whole divided into parts. You can use a circle graph to compare the parts to each other. You can also use it to compare the parts to the whole.

A Circle Graph of Fuel Use

This circle graph shows fuel use in the United States. The graph has 10 equal parts, or sections. Each section equals $\frac{1}{10}$ of the whole. One whole equals $\frac{10}{10}$.

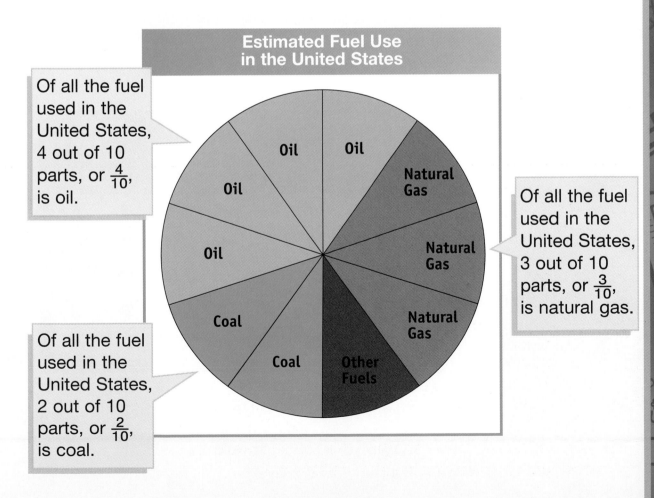

Of all the fuel used in the United States, 4 out of 10 parts, or $\frac{4}{10}$, is oil.

Of all the fuel used in the United States, 2 out of 10 parts, or $\frac{2}{10}$, is coal.

Of all the fuel used in the United States, 3 out of 10 parts, or $\frac{3}{10}$, is natural gas.

Measuring
Elapsed Time

A calendar can help you find out how much time has passed, or elapsed, in days or weeks. A clock can help you see how much time has elapsed in hours and minutes. A clock with a second hand or a stopwatch can help you find out how many seconds have elapsed.

Using a Calendar to Find Elapsed Days

This is a calendar for the month of October. October has 31 days. Suppose it is October 22 and you begin an experiment. You need to check the experiment two days from the start date and one week from the start date. That means you would check it on Wednesday, October 24, and again on Monday, October 29. October 29 is 7 days after October 22.

Monday, Tuesday, Wednesday, Thursday, and Friday are weekdays. Saturday and Sunday are weekends.

Last month ended on Sunday, September 30.

October

Sunday	Monday	Tuesday	Wednesday	Thursday	Friday	Saturday
	1	2	3	4	5	6
7	8	9	10	11	12	13
14	15	16	17	18	19	20
21	22	23	24	25	26	27
28	29	30	31			

Next month begins on Thursday, November 1.

Using a Clock or a Stopwatch to Find Elapsed Time

You need to time an experiment for 20 minutes.

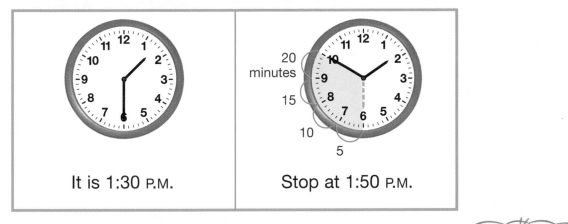

It is 1:30 P.M.   Stop at 1:50 P.M.

You need to time an experiment for 15 seconds. You can use the second hand of a clock or watch.

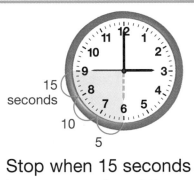

60 seconds = 1 minute

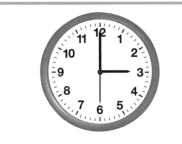

Start the experiment when the second hand is on number 6.

Stop when 15 seconds have passed and the second hand is on the 9.

You can use a stopwatch.

Press the reset button on a stopwatch so that you see 0:00₀₀.

Press the start button. When you see 0:15₀₀, press the stop button.

MEASUREMENTS

Volume
1 L of sports drink is a little more than 1 qt.

Area
A basketball court covers about 4,700 ft². It covers about 435 m².

Mass and Weight
A basketball has a mass of about 650 g. It weighs about 1½ lb.

Metric Measures

Temperature
Ice melts at 0 degrees Celsius (°C)

Water freezes at 0°C

Water boils at 100°C

Length and Distance
1,000 meters (m) = 1 kilometer (km)

100 centimeters (cm) = 1 m

10 millimeters (mm) = 1 cm

Force
1 newton (N) =
   1 kilogram x meter/second/second
   (kg x m/s²)

Volume
1 cubic meter (m³) = 1 m x 1 m x 1 m

1 cubic centimeter (cm³) =
   1 cm x 1 cm x 1 cm

1 liter (L) = 1,000 milliliters (mL)

1 cm³ = 1 mL

Area
1 square kilometer (km²) = 1 km x 1 km

1 hectare = 10,000 m²

Mass
1,000 grams (g) = 1 kilogram (kg)

1,000 milligrams (mg) = 1 g

Temperature
The temperature at an indoor basketball game might be 25°C, which is 77°F.

Length/Distance
A basketball rim is about 10 ft high, or a little more than 3 m from the floor.

Customary Measures

Temperature
Ice melts at 32 degrees Fahrenheit (°F)

Water freezes at 32°F

Water boils at 212°F

Length and Distance
12 inches (in.) = 1 foot (ft)

3 ft = 1 yard (yd)

5,280 ft = 1 mile (mi)

Weight
16 ounces (oz) = 1 pound (lb)

2,000 pounds = 1 ton (T)

Volume of Fluids
8 fluid ounces (fl oz) = 1 cup (c)

2 c = 1 pint (pt)

2 pt = 1 quart (qt)

4 qt = 1 gallon (gal)

Metric and Customary Rates
km/h = kilometers per hour

m/s = meters per second

mph = miles per hour

GLOSSARY

Pronunciation Key

Symbol	Key Words	Symbol	Key Words
a	cat	g	get
ā	ape	h	help
ä	cot, car	j	jump
		k	kiss, call
e	ten, berry	l	leg
ē	me	m	meat
		n	nose
i	fit, here	p	put
ī	ice, fire	r	red
		s	see
ō	go	t	top
ô	fall, for	v	vat
oi	oil	w	wish
͝oo	look, pull	y	yard
o͞o	tool, rule	z	zebra
ou	out, crowd		
		ch	chin, arch
u	up	ŋ	ring, drink
ʉ	fur, shirt	sh	she, push
		th	thin, truth
ə	a in ago	*th*	then, father
	e in agent	zh	measure
	i in pencil		
	o in atom		
	u in circus		

A heavy stress mark (′) is placed after a syllable that gets a heavy, or primary, stress, as in **picture** (pik′chər).

b	bed
d	dog
f	fall

A

adaptation (ad əp tā′shən) A part or behavior that makes a living thing better able to survive in its environment. (C54) The spider's behavior of spinning a web to catch an insect, such as a bee, is an *adaptation* that helps the spider get food

air (er) The invisible, odorless, and tasteless mixture of gases that surrounds Earth. (E10) *Air* consists mainly of the gases nitrogen and oxygen.

air mass (er mas) A large body of air that has about the same temperature, air pressure, and moisture throughout. (E62) When warm and cold *air masses* meet, the weather changes.

air pressure (er presh′ər) The push of the air in all directions against its surroundings. (E31) You can see the effect of *air pressure* when you blow up a balloon.

amphibian (am fib′ē ən) A vertebrate that usually lives in water in the early part of its life; it breathes with gills and then later develops lungs. (C19) Frogs, toads, and salamanders are *amphibians*.

anemometer (an ə mäm′ət ər) A device used to measure the speed of the wind. (E39) The *anemometer* showed that the wind was blowing at 33 km/h.

atmosphere (at′məs fir) The blanket of air that surrounds Earth, reaching to about 700 km above the surface. (E12) Earth's *atmosphere* makes it possible for life to exist on the planet.

atom (at'əm) The smallest part of an element that still has the properties of that element. (B30) Water forms when *atoms* of the elements hydrogen and oxygen combine in a certain way.

axis (ak'sis) An imaginary straight line from the North Pole, through Earth's center, to the South Pole. (E78) Earth makes one complete turn on its *axis* in about 24 hours.

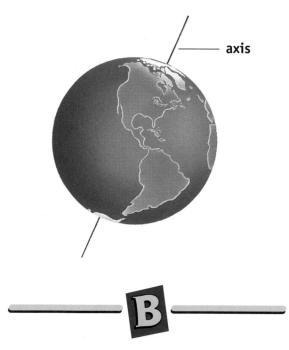

axis

barometer (bə räm'ət ər) A device used to measure air pressure. (E30) Scientists use a *barometer* to gather information about the weather.

bay (bā) Part of a sea or lake extending into the land. (A14) The ship sailed through the *bay* into the Atlantic Ocean.

behavior (bē hāv'yər) The way in which a living thing acts or responds to its environment. (C55) Purring, washing themselves, and hunting mice are three common *behaviors* of cats.

bird (burd) A vertebrate that has wings, is covered with feathers, and hatches from a hard-shell egg. (C21) A *bird* is the only organism in the animal kingdom that has feathers covering its body.

boiling (boil'iŋ) The rapid change of state from a liquid to a gas. (B40) When water is *boiling*, bubbles of water vapor form.

carbon dioxide (kär'bən dī-äks'īd) A colorless, odorless gas. (E10) Plants use *carbon dioxide* from the air in the process of making food.

chemical change (kem'i kəl chānj) A change in matter that results in one or more different kinds of matter forming. (B56) A *chemical change* occurs when matter, such as paper, burns and forms gases and ash.

chemical formula (kem′i kəl fôr′my$\overline{oo}$ lə) A group of symbols that shows the kinds and number of atoms in a single unit of a compound. (B35) The *chemical formula* for carbon dioxide is CO_2.

chemical property (kem′i kəl präp′ər tē) A characteristic of a substance that can only be seen when the substance changes and a new substance is formed; describes how matter reacts with other matter. (B13, B56) A *chemical property* of iron is that iron can combine with oxygen to form rust.

chemical reaction (kem′i kəl rē ak′shən) The process in which one or more substances are changed into one or more different substances. (B57) A *chemical reaction* takes place when burning wood changes to ash.

chemical symbol (kem′i kəl sim′bəl) One or two letters that stand for the name of an element. (B30) The *chemical symbol* for gold is *Au*.

circuit breaker (sʉr′kit brāk′ər) A switch that opens or closes a circuit by turning off or on. (D52) When a circuit overheats, the *circuit breaker* switches off and the lights go out.

cirrus cloud (sir′əs kloud) A thin, feathery cloud made up of ice crystals high in the sky. (E57) *Cirrus clouds* often look like wisps of hair.

climate (klī′mət) The average weather conditions of an area over a long period of time. (E84) Some regions have a hot, rainy *climate*.

cloud (kloud) A mass of tiny droplets of water that condensed from the air. (E46) A dark *cloud* blocked the sunlight.

cold front (kōld frunt) The leading edge of a cold air mass that forms as the cold air mass moves into a warm air mass. (E62) Thunderstorms often occur along a *cold front*.

compass (kum′pəs) A device containing a magnetized needle that moves freely and is used to show direction. (D23) The north pole of the needle in a *compass* points toward Earth's magnetic north pole.

compound (käm′pound)
Matter made up of two or more elements chemically combined. (B33) Salt is a *compound* made up of sodium and chlorine.

condensation (kän dən sā′shən)
The change of state from a gas to a liquid. (B42) Drops of water form on the outside of a very cold glass because of the *condensation* of water vapor in the air.

condense (kən dens′) To change from a gas to a liquid. (E46) Water vapor from the air *condenses* on a cold window.

conductor (kən duk′tər) A material through which electricity moves easily. (D42) Copper wire is a good *conductor* of electricity.

conifers (kän′ə fərz) Cone-bearing plants. (C37) Pines and fir trees are examples of *conifers*.

conservation (kän sər vā′shən)
The preserving and wise use of natural resources. (A31) The *conservation* of forests is important to both humans and wildlife.

controlled experiment (kən-trōld′ ek sper′ə mənt) A test of a hypothesis in which the setups are identical in all ways except one. (S7) In the *controlled experiment*, one beaker of water contained salt.

cumulus cloud (kyo͞o′myo͞o ləs kloud) A large puffy cloud. (E55) White *cumulus clouds* can often be seen in an otherwise clear summer sky.

delta (del′tə) A flat, usually triangular plain formed by deposits of sediment where a river empties into the ocean. (A12) The largest *delta* in the United States is at the mouth of the Mississippi River.

density (den′sə tē) The property that describes how much matter is in a given space, or volume. (B9, B11) The *density* of air varies with its temperature.

dicot (dī′kät) A flowering plant that produces seeds that have two sections. (C38) A trait of a *dicot* is that the veins of its leaves form a branching pattern.

electric cell (ē lek′trik sel) A device that changes chemical energy to electrical energy. (D60) A battery in a flashlight consists of one or more *electric cells*.

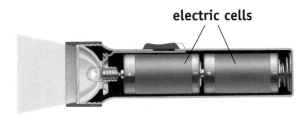

electric cells

electric charge (ē lek′trik chärj) The electrical property of particles of matter; an electric charge can be positive or negative. (D30) Rubbing a balloon with a wool cloth causes negative *electric charges* to move from the wool to the balloon.

electric circuit (ē lek′trik sur′kit) A path along which an electric current can move. (D41) We made an *electric circuit,* using a battery, wires, and a light bulb.

electric current (ē lek′trik kur′ənt) A continuous flow of electric charges. (D41) *Electric current* in wires allows you to run electric appliances, such as an iron or refrigerator, in your home.

electric discharge (ē lek′trik dis′chärj) The loss or release of an electric charge. (D33) A bolt of lightning is an *electric discharge*.

electromagnet (ē lek′trō mag nit) A magnet made when an electric current passes through a wire coiled around an iron core. (D70) A large *electromagnet* can be strong enough to lift heavy metal objects such as cars.

element (el′ə mənt) Matter made up of only one kind of atom. (B30) Iron, oxygen, and aluminum are three examples of *elements*.

energy (en′ər jē) The ability to cause change. (B39) Most automobiles use *energy* from gasoline to move.

environment (en vī′rən mənt) Everything that surrounds and affects a living thing. (C44) Desert animals and forest animals live in very different *environments*.

equator (ē kwāt′ər) An imaginary line circling the middle of Earth, halfway between the North Pole and the South Pole. (E78) The *equator* divides Earth into the Northern Hemisphere and the Southern Hemisphere.

erosion (ē rō′zhən) The gradual wearing away and removing of rock material by forces such as moving water, wind, and moving ice. (A10) Ocean waves cause *erosion* of the seashore.

evaporate (ē vap′ə rāt) To change from a liquid to a gas. (E46) Some of the water boiling in the pot *evaporated*.

evaporation (ē vap ə rā′shən) The change of state from a liquid to a gas. (B40) Under the hot sun, water in a puddle changes to water vapor through the process of *evaporation*.

exoskeleton (eks ō skel′ə tən) A hard outer structure, such as a shell, that protects or supports an animal's body. (C15) A lobster has a thick *exoskeleton*.

extinct (ek stiŋkt′) No longer living as a species. (C58) Traces of some *extinct* species can be found in fossils.

ferns (fʉrnz) Spore-forming plants that have roots, stems, and leaves. (C36) *Ferns* that grow in tropical places have very tall fronds.

filament (fil′ə mənt) A long, thin coil of wire that glows when electricity passes through it. (D48) The *filament* in an incandescent light bulb gives off light.

filament

fish (fish) A vertebrate that lives in water and has gills used for breathing and fins used for swimming. (C18) Sharks and tuna are kinds of *fish*.

flash flood (flash flud) A sudden, violent flood. (E67) Heavy rains caused *flash floods* as the stream overflowed.

fog (fôg) A cloud that touches Earth's surface. (E46) Traffic accidents often increase where *fog* is heavy.

fossil fuel (fäs′əl fyo͞o′əl) A fuel that formed from the remains of once-living things and that is nonrenewable. (A47) Oil is a *fossil fuel*.

freezing (frēz′iŋ) The change of state from a liquid to a solid. (B42) Water turns to ice by *freezing*.

front (frunt) The place where two air masses meet. (E62) Forecasters watch the movement of *fronts* to help predict the weather.

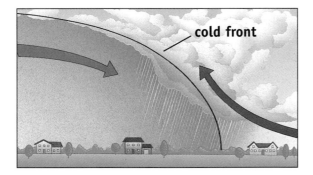

cold front

fuse (fyo͞oz) A device in a circuit that contains a metal strip, which melts when the circuit is overheated, thus breaking the circuit. (D52) The *fuse* blew because too many appliances were connected to the same electric circuit.

gas (gas) The state of matter that has no definite shape or volume. (B29) Helium is a very light *gas* that is used to fill some balloons.

generator (jen′ər āt ər) A device that changes energy of motion into electrical energy. (D58) The huge *generator* uses water power to produce electricity.

gill (gil) A feathery structure on each side of a fish's head that lets the fish breathe underwater. (C18) A fish takes in oxygen through its *gills*.

glacier (glā′shər) A huge mass of slow-moving ice that forms over land; glaciers form in areas where the amount of snow that falls is more than the amount of snow that melts. (A22) As it moves, a *glacier* changes the surface beneath it.

greenhouse effect (grēn′hous e fekt′) The process by which heat from the Sun builds up near Earth's surface and is trapped by the atmosphere. (E15) Some scientists fear that air pollution may increase the *greenhouse effect* and raise temperatures on Earth.

hazardous waste (haz′ər dəs wāst) A waste material that dirties the environment and that can kill living things or cause disease. (A65) Some chemicals used to kill insects become *hazardous wastes*.

headland (hed′land) A piece of land that extends out into the water and usually slows down the flow of water that passes it. (A14) The lighthouse stood on a *headland* overlooking the bay.

high-pressure area (hī presh′ər er′ē ə) An area of higher air pressure than that of the surrounding air. (E33) Winds move from *high-pressure areas* to low-pressure areas.

horsetails (hôrs tālz) Plants that reproduce by spores and have underground stems. (C36) *Horsetails* are also known as scouring rushes because of the tough tip at the end of their bamboo-like stem.

humidity (hyo͞o mid′ə tē) The amount of water vapor in the air. (E47) Tropical climates have warm temperatures and high *humidity*.

hurricane (hʉr′i kān) A large, violent storm accompanied by strong winds and, usually, heavy rain. (E70) The winds of the *hurricane* blew at over 125 km/h.

hypothesis (hī päth′ə sis) An idea about or explanation of how or why something happens. (S6) The *hypothesis* about the expanding universe has been supported by evidence gathered by astronomers.

ice age (īs āj) A period of time when glaciers covered much of Earth's land. (E89) During the last *ice age,* glaciers covered parts of North America.

incineration (in sin ər ā′shən) Burning to ashes. (A60) You can get rid of trash by *incineration*.

instinctive behavior (in stiŋk′tiv bē hāv′yər) A behavior that a living thing does naturally without having to learn it. (C56) For a mother bird, feeding her young is an *instinctive behavior*.

insulator (in′sə lāt ər) A material through which electricity does not move easily. (D42) Rubber can prevent an electric shock because rubber is a good *insulator*.

invertebrate (in vʉr′tə brit) An animal that does not have a backbone. (C15) *Invertebrates* include jellyfish, sponges, insects, and worms.

landfill (land'fil) An area where trash is buried and covered over with dirt. (A59) In some places, towns decide to build recreation areas, such as parks, on the sites of old *landfills*.

learned behavior (lʉrnd bē-hāv'yər) A behavior that an organism is taught or learns from experience. (C56) Sitting on command, catching a ball, and jumping through a hoop are examples of *learned behavior* for a dog.

lines of force (līnz uv fôrs) The lines that form a pattern showing the size and shape of a magnetic force field. (D19) Iron filings sprinkled over a magnet form *lines of force* that show the strength and the direction of the magnet's force.

liquid (lik'wid) The state of matter that has a definite volume but no definite shape. (B29) A *liquid*, such as water or milk, takes the shape of its container.

litter (lit'ər) The trash that is discarded on the ground or in water rather than being disposed of properly. (A66) The children cleaned up the park by removing all the *litter* they could find.

liverworts (liv'ər wʉrts) Nonseed plants that lack true roots, stems, and leaves. (C36) The logs by the stream were covered with mosslike *liverworts*.

lodestone (lōd'stōn) A naturally magnetic mineral found at or near Earth's surface. (D22) A piece of *lodestone* will attract iron.

low-pressure area (lō presh'ər er'ē ə) An area of lower air pressure than that of the surrounding air. (E33) Storms are more likely to occur in *low-pressure areas*.

magnet (mag'nit) An object that has the property of attracting certain materials, mainly iron and steel. (D11) The girl used a horseshoe *magnet* to pick up paper clips.

magnetic field (mag net'ik fēld) The space around a magnet within which the force of the magnet can act. (D20) The magnet attracted all the pins within its *magnetic field*.

magnetism (mag′nə tiz əm) A magnet's property of attracting certain materials, mainly iron and steel. (D11) *Magnetism* keeps kitchen magnets attached to a refrigerator door.

mammal (mam′əl) A vertebrate, such as a cat, that has hair or fur and feeds its young with milk. (C22) Dogs, cats, rabbits, deer, bats, horses, mice, elephants, whales, and humans are all *mammals*.

mass (mas) The amount of matter that something contains. (B10) A large rock has more *mass* than a small rock that is made of the same material.

matter (mat′ər) Anything that has mass and takes up space. (B10) Rocks, water, and air are three kinds of *matter*.

melting (melt′iŋ) The change of state from a solid to a liquid. (B40) As the temperature of the air rises, snow and ice change to liquid water by the process of *melting*.

metric system (me′trik sis′təm) A system of measurement in which the number of smaller parts in each unit is based on the number 10 and multiples of 10. (B20) Centimeters, meters, and kilometers are units of length in the *metric system*.

mineral (min′ər əl) A solid, found in nature, that has a definite chemical makeup. (A41) Salt, coal, diamond, and gold are some examples of *minerals*.

mixture (miks′chər) Matter that is made up of two or more substances that can be separated by physical means. (B50) This salad contains a *mixture* of lettuce, cucumbers, celery, and tomatoes.

molt (mōlt) To shed an outer covering such as hair, outer skin, horns, or feathers at certain times. (C30) Snakes and insects *molt*.

monocot (män′ō kät) A flowering plant that produces seeds that are in one piece. (C38) About one third of all flowering plants are *monocots*.

mosses (môs′əs) Small nonseed plants that lack true roots, stems, and leaves. (C35) The leaflike part of *mosses* grows only a few centimeters above ground.

natural resource (nach′ər əl
rē′sôrs) Any useful material from
Earth, such as water, oil, and minerals. (A31) One reason that trees are
an important *natural resource* is
that their wood is used to build
houses and to make paper.

nitrogen (nī′trə jən) A colorless,
odorless, tasteless gas that makes up
about four fifths of the air. (E10)
Nitrogen is used by plants for
growth.

nonrenewable resource (nän-
ri nōō′ə bəl rē′sôrs) A natural
resource that can't be replaced once
it's removed. (A42) Minerals are
classified as a *nonrenewable
resource* because there's a limited
amount of them.

nonseed plants (nän sēd plants)
Plants that do not reproduce with
seeds. (C35) Ferns are *nonseed
plants.*

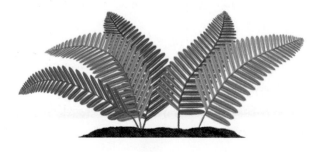

Northern Hemisphere
(nôr′thərn hem′i sfir) The half of
Earth north of the equator. (E79)
Canada is in the *Northern
Hemisphere.*

north pole (nôrth pōl) One of the
ends of a magnet where the magnetic
force is strongest; it points to the
north when the magnet moves freely.
(D13) *North poles* of magnets repel
each other.

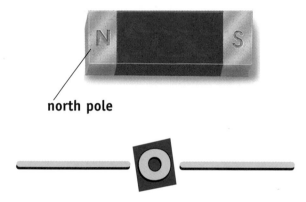

north pole

ore (ôr) A mineral or rock that
contains enough of a metal to make
mining that metal profitable. (A41)
Gold, aluminum, copper, and tin
come from *ores.*

organism (ôr′gə niz əm) A living
thing that can be classified as belong-
ing to one of several kingdoms. (C8)
Animals and plants are *organisms.*

oxygen (äks′i jən) A colorless,
odorless, tasteless gas that makes up
about one fifth of the air. (E10)
Oxygen is essential to life.

packaging (pak'ij iŋ) The wrapping and containers in which items are transported or offered for sale. (A75) *Packaging* protects products from damage but adds to their cost.

parallel circuit (par'ə lel sʉr'kit) An electric circuit having more than one path along which electric current can travel. (D51) Because the circuits in a home are *parallel circuits*, you can switch off one light and others will stay on.

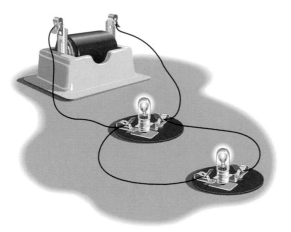

physical change (fiz'i kəl chānj) A change in size, shape, or state of matter in which no new matter is formed. (B48) Cutting an apple in half and freezing water into ice cubes are *physical changes*.

physical property (fiz'i kəl präp'ər tē) A characteristic of a material or object that can be seen or measured without changing the material into a new substance. (B12) One *physical property* of a ball is its round shape.

polar climate (pō'lər klī'mət) A very cold climate that does not receive much energy from the Sun. (E85) The Arctic has a *polar climate*.

pollutant (pə loot'ʼnt) A substance that causes pollution. (A65) The exhaust gases from cars add *pollutants* to the air.

pollution (pə loo'shən) The dirtying of the environment with waste materials or other unwanted substances. (A65) Water *pollution* can cause disease or even death in living things.

precipitation (prē sip ə tā'shən) Any form of water that falls from clouds to Earth's surface. (E46) Rain, snow, and hail are forms of *precipitation*.

property (präp'ər tē) A characteristic that describes matter. (B12) Hardness is a *property* of steel.

rain gauge (rān gāj) A device for measuring precipitation. (E47) The *rain gauge* at the weather station showed that 2 cm of rain had fallen in 24 hours.

recycle (rē sī′kəl) To process and reuse materials. (A72) Discarded newspapers are *recycled* to make new paper.

relative humidity (rel′ə tiv hyo͞o mid′ə tē) The amount of water vapor present in the air at a given temperature compared to the maximum amount that the air could hold at that temperature. (E47) A *relative humidity* of 95 percent on a warm day can make you feel sticky and uncomfortable.

renewable resource (ri no͞o′ə-bəl rē′sôrs) A resource that can be replaced. (A42) Water is a *renewable resource* because rain increases the supply of water.

reptile (rep′təl) A vertebrate, such as a lizard or a crocodile, that has dry scaly skin and lays eggs that have a leathery shell. (C20) *Reptiles* can be found in both deserts and rain forests.

river system (riv′ər sis′təm) A river and all the waterways, such as brooks, streams, and rivers, that drain into it. (A11) The Mississippi River and the many waterways feeding into it make up the largest *river system* in the country.

rock (räk) A solid material that is made up of one or more minerals and that may be used for its properties. (A41) Granite is a hard *rock* used in construction.

sand dune (sand do͞on) A mound, hill, or ridge of sand formed by the wind. (A21) *Sand dunes* are common in the desert.

sand dune

savanna (sə van′ə) A broad, grassy plain that has few or no trees. (C48) Nearly half of Africa is covered by *savannas*.

sediment (sed'ə mənt) Sand, soil, and rock carried by water, wind, or ice. (A12) The rushing water of the river deposited *sediment* along the riverbanks.

seed plants (sēd plants) Plants that reproduce with seeds. (C35) Corn and wheat are *seed plants*.

series circuit (sir'ēz sur'kit) An electric circuit in which the parts are connected in a single path. (D50) Electric current can follow only one path in a *series circuit*.

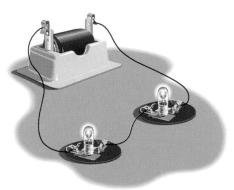

soil (soil) Loose material that covers much of Earth's land surface and is made up of three layers—topsoil, subsoil, and partly weathered rock. (A30) Plants, insects, and worms live in *soil*.

solar cell (sō'lər sel) A device that changes sunlight into electrical energy. (D64) *Solar cells* used in power plants can produce electricity without polluting the air.

solar energy (sō'lər en'ər jē) The clean and relatively low-cost energy from the Sun. (A50, D64) *Solar energy* is used to heat water in some homes.

solid (säl'id) Matter that has a definite volume and a definite shape. (B29) A *solid*, such as a rock, a wooden block, or an ice cube, has a definite volume and shape.

solution (sə lōō'shən) A mixture in which the particles of different substances are mixed evenly. (B51) Stirring sugar into water makes a *solution*.

Southern Hemisphere (su*th*'ərn hem'i sfir) The half of Earth south of the equator. (E79) The island continent Australia is in the *Southern Hemisphere*.

south pole (south pōl) One of the ends of a magnet where the magnetic force is strongest; it points to the south when the magnet moves freely. (D13) The *south pole* of one magnet attracts the north pole of another magnet.

standard unit (stan'dərd yōōn'it) A unit of measure that everyone agrees to use. (B19) Scientists use the gram as the *standard unit* of mass.

state of matter (stāt uv mat'ər) Any of the three forms that matter may ordinarily take: solid, liquid, and gas. (B29) When ice melts, it changes to a liquid *state of matter.*

static electricity (stat'ik ē lek-tris'i tē)) Electric charges that have built up on the surface of an object. (D31) Walking across a carpet on a cold, dry day can produce *static electricity.*

stratus cloud (strāt'əs kloud) A low, flat cloud that often brings drizzle. (E55) Large sheets of very dark *stratus clouds* covered the sky on the rainy morning.

substance (sub'stəns) A class of matter made up of elements and compounds. (B34) Salt and sugar are *substances.*

switch (swich) A device that completes or breaks the path a current can follow in an electric circuit. (D41) In order to turn on the light, you must press the *switch* to complete the circuit.

temperate climate (tem'pər it klī'mət) A climate that generally has warm, dry summers and cold, wet winters. (E85) Most regions of the United States have a *temperate climate.*

theory (thē'ə rē) A hypothesis that is supported by a lot of evidence and is widely accepted by scientists. (S9) The big-bang *theory* offers an explanation for the origin of the universe.

thunderstorm (thun'dər stôrm) A storm that produces lightning and thunder and often heavy rain and strong winds. (E66) When the weather is hazy, hot, and humid, *thunderstorms* are likely to develop.

tornado (tôr nā'dō) A violent, funnel-shaped storm of spinning wind. (E72) The wind speed at the center of a *tornado* can be twice that of hurricane winds.

tropical climate (träp'i kəl klī'mət) A hot, rainy climate. (E85) Areas that are near the equator have a *tropical climate* because they receive the greatest amount of energy from the Sun.

troposphere (trō′pō sfir) The layer of the atmosphere closest to the surface of Earth. (E12) The *troposphere* reaches about 11 km above the surface of Earth and is the layer of the atmosphere in which weather occurs.

variable (ver′ē ə bəl) The one difference in the setups of a controlled experiment; provides a comparison for testing a hypothesis. (S7) The *variable* in an experiment with plants was the amount of water given each plant.

vertebra (vʉr′tə brə) One of the bones that together make up the backbone. (C14) Each knob in your backbone is a *vertebra*.

vertebrate (vʉr′tə brit) An animal that has a backbone. (C14) Reptiles and birds are *vertebrates*.

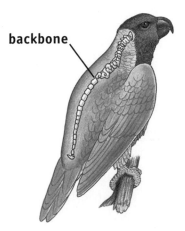

backbone

voltage (vōl′tij) The force of an electric current, measured in volts. (D63) Electric currents of high *voltage* travel through long-distance power lines.

volume (văl yōōm) The amount of space that matter takes up. (B10) A baseball has a greater *volume* than a golf ball does.

warm front (wôrm frunt) The leading edge of a warm air mass that forms as the warm air mass moves forward into a cold air mass. (E63) Light rain often falls along a *warm front*.

water cycle (wôt′ər si′kəl) The movement of water into the air as water vapor and back to Earth's surface as rain, snow, or hail. (E46) The *water cycle* is powered by energy from the Sun.

water vapor (wôt′ər vā′pər) Water that is in the form of a gas. (E10) *Water vapor* from the air forms drops of water on cold glass surfaces.

weather (we*th*′ər) The condition of the atmosphere at a certain place and time. (E13) The *weather* today in Chicago is snowy.

weather forecaster (we*th*'ər fôr'kast ər) A person who makes weather predictions or reports weather conditions. (E61) The *weather forecaster* predicted rain for the next three days.

weather satellite (we*th*'ər sat''l īt) A human-made device in space that takes pictures of Earth and collects information about the weather. (E54) The *weather satellite* sent back pictures of clouds to weather stations in different locations on the ground.

weathering (we*th*'ər iŋ) The physical and chemical processes by which rock is broken down into smaller pieces. (A10) Cracks in rock produced by freezing rainwater or the growth of plant roots are examples of *weathering*.

wind (wind) The movement of air over Earth's surface. (E21) The strong *wind* lifted the kite high above the houses.

windsock (wind'säk) A device used to show wind direction, consisting of a cloth bag that is open at both ends and hung on a pole. (E38) The *windsock* showed that the wind was blowing from the north.

wind vane (wind vān) A device, often shaped like an arrow, used to show the direction of the wind. (E38) The *wind vane* on the roof of the weather station showed that the wind was blowing from the southwest.

INDEX

* **Activity**

CREDITS

ILLUSTRATORS
Cover: Genine Smith.

Think Like a Scientist: 14: Laurie Hamilton. *Border:* Genine Smith.

Unit A: 11, 13: Susan Johnston Carlson. 13–15: Paul Mirocha. 22–24: Jim Turgeon. 23, 25: Skip Baker. 30–31: Brad Gaber. 32–33: Jim Salvati. 38–39: Dave Joly. 39: Eldon Doty. 40: Brad Gaber. 43: Terry Ravenelli. 44: Terry Boles. 46: Rodica Prato. 47: Martucci Studio. 51: Brad Gaber. 56: Jim Trusilo. 58–59: Robert Roper. 61: Ray Vella. 63: Michael Ingle. 64: Greg Harris. 65: Robert Roper. 68: Greg Harris. 69–71: Bob Ostrom. 71: Eldon Doty. 72–74: Scott MacNeil. 76: Ken Bowser. 77: Randy Chewning.

Unit B: 12–13: Nina Laden. 18: Dave Winter. 19: Terry Boles. 19–22: Mark Bender. 29–31: J.A.K. Graphics. 32: Susan Johnston Carlson. 33: Tom Buches. 34–35: J.A.K. Graphics. 38, 40–41: Ron Fleming. 43: J.A.K. Graphics. 49: Andrew Shiff. 53: Patrick Gnan. 59: Bob Doucet. 60: Dartmouth Publishing.

Unit C: 8–9: Lee Steadman. 12–13: Susan Melrath. 13: Linda Warner. 13: Eldon Doty. 14–15: Dave Barber. 18–20: Jim Deal. 30: Barbara Hoopes Ambler. 35: Wendy Smith-Griswold. 40–41: Phil Wilson. 44: Jackie Urbanovic. 44–47: Julie Tsuchya. 48–49: Linda Howard. 54–57: Richard Cowdrey. 59–60: Randy Hamblin.

Unit D: 13: Patrick Gnan. 15: Dan McGowan. 22: Brad Gaber. 30–31: Robert Roper. 35: *t.* Jim Effier; *m.* Andrew Shiff. 40: David Winter. 41: Hans & Cassady, Inc. 42–43: Dale Gustafson. 48: Patrick Gnan. 50–51: Hans & Cassady, Inc. 52: Robert Roper. 53: Hans & Cassady, Inc. 60–61: Robert Roper. 62–63: Geoffrey McCormick. 68–69: Vincent Wayne. 70, 72: Robert Roper. 74–76: Michael Sloan.

Unit E: 11, 13: Randy Hamblin. 14–15: Robert Roper. 20: Andy Lendway. 22: Flora Jew. 23: Robert Roper. 30: Susan Melrath. 31: Rob Burger. 32: Tom Pansini. 33: Rob Burger. 38–39: Pamela Becker. 46: Michael Kline. 49: Rob Burger. 55: Gary Torrisi. 56: Patrick Gnan. 60: Kristin Kest. 60: Thomas Cranmer. 61–63: Nancy Tobin. 62: Robert Roper. 66, 68–70: Tom Lochray. 71: Gary Torrisi. 72: Tom Lochray. 73: Gary Torrisi. 77: Josie Yee. 78: Mike Quon. 79: Josie Yee. 80–81: John Youssi. 84–85: Thomas Cranmer. 86–87: Uldis Klavins. 90–92: Julie Peterson. 93: John Youssi.

Math and Science Toolbox: *Logos:* Nancy Tobin. 14–15: Andrew Shiff. *Borders:* Genine Smith.

Glossary 17: *t.r.* Dan McGowan. *m.l.* Richard Cowdrey. *b.r.* Dale Gustafson. 18: Mike Quon. 19: Dale Gustafson. 20: Dan McGowan. 21,22: Dale Gustafson. 23: Robert Roper. 24: A.J. Miller. 26,27: Patrick Gnan. 28: Hans & Cassady Inc. 29: Dan McGowan. 30: Hans & Cassady Inc. 32: David Barber. 33: Patrick Gnan.

PHOTOGRAPHS
All photographs by Houghton Mifflin Co. (HMCo.) unless otherwise noted.

Front Cover: *t.* Superstock; *m.l.* Bill Brooks/Masterfile Corporation; *m.r.* Tim Flach/Tony Stone Images; *b.l.* Barbara Leslie/FPG International; *b.r.* Greg Ryan & Sally Beyer/Tony Stone Images.

Table of Contents iv: *l.* Harold Sund/The Image Bank; *r.* Cromosohm/Sohm/The Stock Market. viii: Stan Osolinski/The Stock Market. xiii: *t.r.* Brian Parker/Tom Stack & Associates; *b.l.* Tony Freeman/PhotoEdit; *b.m.* Buff Corsi/Tom Stack & Associates; *b.r.* Gary Withey/Bruce Coleman Incorporated. xiv: © 2000 Juha Jormanainen/Woodfin Camp & Associates. xv: *l.* NOAA; *r.* NOAA/NESDIS/NCDC/SDSD.

Think Like a Scientist: 2: *t. bkgd.* PhotoDisc, Inc. 3: *t.* PhotoDisc, Inc. 4–5: *bkgd.* Chip Henderson Photography.

Unit A 1: Kim Heacox/Tony Stone Images. 2–3: Kim Heacox/Tony Stone Images. 4: Mark Hopkins. 4–5: *bkgd.* Miriam Romais; *m.t.* Miriam Romais; *t.* Miriam Romais; *m.b.* Miriam Romais; *b.* Miriam Romais. 10: *l.* E.R. Degginger/Color-Pic, Inc.; *m.* C.C. Lockwood/DRK Photo; *r.* Cameron Davidson/Comstock. 12: *l.* Tom Stack & Associates; *r.* Manfred Gottschalk/Tom Stack & Associates. 13: Scott Blackman/Tom Stack & Associates. 14: *l.* E.R. Degginger/Color-Pic, Inc.; *r.* NASA/Corbis Media. 15: Bob Daemmrich Photography. 20–21: *bkgd.* Larry Ulrich/DRK Photo; *inset* Breck P. Kent Photography. 21: Breck P. Kent Photography. 22: *l.* E.R. Degginger/Color-

Pic, Inc.; *r.* Breck P. Kent Photography. 22–23: © Porterfield/Chickering/Photo Researchers, Inc. 24: Spencer Swanger/Tom Stack & Associates. 26–27: *bkgd.* Richard Hamilton Smith/Corbis Corporation; *inset* Thanh H. Dao/USDA-ARS-CPRL. 32: *t.* Harold Sund/The Image Bank; *b.* J.C. Carton/Bruce Coleman Incorporated. 33: *t.* Kevin Schafer/Tom Stack & Associates; *b.* John Callahan/Tony Stone Images. 34: Grant Huntington for HMCo. 36: Grant Huntington for HMCo. 36–37: Grant Huntington for HMCo. 37: Grant Huntington for HMCo. 41: Grant Huntington for HMCo. 43: *t.l.* Edward Bower/The Image Bank; *t.r.* Lester Lefkowitz/Tony Stone Images; *b.l.* Lester Lefkowitz/Tony Stone Images. 49: *t.l.* J. Barry O'Rourke/The Stock Market; *t.r.* J. Barry O'Rourke/The Stock Market; *b.* © Ludek Pesek/Photo Researchers, Inc.; *inset* Mike Abrahams/Tony Stone Images. 50: Cromosohm/Sohm/The Stock Market. 52–53: *bkgd.* Paul Conklin/PhotoEdit; *inset* Robert Holmgren Photography. 64: Frans Lanting/Minden Pictures. 66: Grant Heilman Photography, Inc. 67: *t.* Larry Lefever/Grant Heilman Photography, Inc.; *b.* Runk/Schoenberger/Grant Heilman Photography, Inc. 74: *l.* © Donald S. Heintzelman/Photo Researchers, Inc.; *r.* © Will McIntyre/Photo Researchers, Inc.

Unit B 1: © Vito Palmisano/Photo Researchers, Inc. 2–3: © Vito Palmisano/Photo Researchers, Inc. 4: Melvin Epps/Third Eye Production. 4–5: *bkgd.* Martina Johnson-Allen; *inset* Martina Johnson-Allen. 13: *t.r.* © Milton Heiberg/Photo Researchers, Inc.; *b.r.* David Young-Wolff/PhotoEdit. 24–25: *bkgd.* © Chris Marona/Photo Researchers, Inc.; *inset* Los Alamos National Laboratory. 26: Grant Huntington for HMCo. 27: Grant Huntington for HMCo. 28: *t.* Grant Huntington for HMCo.; *b.* Grant Huntington for HMCo. 29: *l.* Light Images, Inc.; *m.* Al Clayton/International Stock; *r.* Miwako Ikeda/International Stock. 34: Grant Huntington for HMCo. 36: Grant Huntington for HMCo. 37: Grant Huntington for HMCo. 39: Barry L. Runk/Grant Heilman Photgraphy, Inc. 42: *l.* Zefa Germany/The Stock Market; *m.* Greg Ryan & Sally Beyer/Positive Reflections; *r.* Richard Hutchings for HMCo. 46: Grant Huntington for HMCo. 47: Grant Huntington for HMCo. 48: Grant Huntington for HMCo. 48–49: Grant Huntington for HMCo. 50: *t.* Grant Huntington for HMCo.; *b.* Grant Huntington for HMCo. 51: *t.* © George Whitely/Photo Researchers, Inc. 52: Grant Huntington for HMCo. 54: Grant Huntington for HMCo. 55: *t.* Grant Huntington for HMCo.; *b.* Grant Huntington for HMCo. 56–57: John Gurzinski. 57: *l.* Superstock; *r.* Robert Brenner/PhotoEdit. 58: Jim Smalley/The Picture Cube. 59: Grant Huntington for HMCo. 61: *l.* Grant Huntington for HMCo.; *r.* Grant Huntington for HMCo.

Unit C 1: Stuart Westmorland/Tony Stone Images. 2–3: Stuart Westmorland/Tony Stone Images. 4–5: *bkgd.* Inga Spence/Tom Stack & Associates; *inset* Frans Lanting/Minden Pictures. 7: Richard Hutchings for HMCo. 10: *t.l.* © Tom McHugh/Photo Researchers, Inc.; *t.r.* Jane Burton/Bruce Coleman Incorporated; *b.* © Hermann Eisenbeiss/Photo Researchers, Inc. 11: *t.* Dwight R. Kuhn; *m.l.* © Michael Abbey/Photo Researchers, Inc.; *m.r.* © Gary Reterford/Science Source/Photo Researchers, Inc.; *b.l.* Kim Taylor/Bruce Coleman Incorporated; *b.r.* © Biophoto Associates/Science Source/Photo Researchers, Inc. 19: *t. to b.* Dwight R. Kuhn; Donald Specker/Animals Animals/Earth Scenes; E.R. Degginger/Color-Pic, Inc.; Zig Leszczynski/Animals Animals/Earth Scenes; Dwight R. Kuhn. 20: Art Wolfe/Tony Stone Images. 21: *bkgd.* David Sailors/The Stock Market; *l.* G.I. Bernard/Oxford Scientific Films/Animals Animals/Earth Scenes; *inset* Al Hamdan/The Image Bank. 22: *t.* Doug Perrine/DRK Photo; *b.* S. Nielsen/Imagery. 23: © Tom & Pat Leeson/Photo Researchers, Inc. 25: Richard Hutchings for HMCo. 26: *t.* Dwight R. Kuhn; *b.l.* The Granger Collection, New York; *b.r.* B.W. Payton. 27: *bkgd.* Larry Lipsky/Bruce Coleman Incorporated; *inset* M.C. Chamberlain/DRK Photo. 28: *t.* M.C. Chamberlain/DRK Photo; *b.l.* Mike Severns/Tom Stack & Associates; *b.r.* Brian Parker/Tom Stack & Associates. 29: *t.l.* Carl Roessler/Bruce Coleman Incorporated; *t.r.* Carol L. Geake/Animals Animals/Earth Scenes; *b.* Stephen Frink/Corbis Media. 31: *l. to r.* E.R. Degginger/Color-Pic, Inc.; James Cotier/Tony Stone Images; Andrew J. Martinez/Stock Boston; E.R. Degginger/Color-Pic, Inc.; Charles Sleicher/Tony Stone Images; Rosemary Calvert/Tony Stone Images. 32: *l.* © Rod Planck/Photo Researchers, Inc.; *r.* Phil Degginger/Color-Pic, Inc. 34: *t.l.* E.R. Degginger/Color-Pic, Inc.; *t.r.* © Alan & Linda Detrick/Photo Researchers, Inc.; *m.r.* Maximillian Stock/Stock Food America; *b.l.* Ray Pfortner/Peter Arnold, Inc.; *b.r.* E.R. Degginger/Color-Pic, Inc.; *l. inset* Tom & Pat Leeson/DRK Photo; *r. inset* E.R. Degginger/Color-Pic, Inc. 36: *t.l.* Runk/Schoenberger/Grant Heilman Photography, Inc.; *t.r.* © Alvin E. Staffan/Photo Researchers, Inc.; *b.l.* K.G. Preston Mafham/Animals Animals/Earth Scenes; *b.r.* Carl Wolinsky/Stock Boston. 37: *t.l.* © Dan Suzio/Photo Researchers, Inc.; *t.r.* © Dan Suzio/Photo Researchers, Inc. 38: *l.* E.R. Degginger/Color-Pic, Inc. 39: © Tom McHugh/Photo Researchers, Inc. 42: Stan Osolinski/The Stock Market. 43: *t.l.* © Renate & Gerd Wustig/Okapia/Photo Researchers, Inc.; *t.r.* Gary W. Griffen/Animals Animals/Earth Scenes; *b.l.* Robert A. Ross/Color-Pic, Inc.; *b.r.* Fred Bruemmer/DRK Photo. 44: *bkgd.* Spencer Swanger/Tom Stack & Associates; *inset* E.R. Degginger/Color-Pic, Inc. 45: *t.l.* Fred Fellerman/Tony Stone Images; *t.r.* Peter Drowne/Color-Pic, Inc.; *b.* Robert Maier/Animals Animals/Earth Scenes. 46: *t.* John Cancalosi/Tom Stack & Associates; *b.l.* R.J.B. Goodale/Animals Animals/Earth Scenes; *b.r.* M.C. Chamberlin/DRK Photo. 47: © Craig K. Lorenz/Photo Researchers, Inc. 54: *l.* © Cosmos Blank/National Audubon Society/Photo Researchers, Inc. 55: *l.* M. Austerman/Animals Animals/Earth Scenes; *r.* C.C. Lockwood/Animals Animals/Earth Scenes. 56: *t.* © M. Reardon/Photo Researchers, Inc.; *b.* Charlie Palek/Animals Animals/Earth Scenes. 57: *t.* Rod Planck/Tony Stone Images. 59: CNP/Archive Photos. 61: C.C. Lockwood/Animals Animals/Earth Scenes.

Unit D 1: Kennan Ward/The Stock Market. 2–3: Kennan Ward/The Stock Market. 4–5: *bkgd.* © Thomas Porett/Photo Researchers, Inc.; *inset* Grace Moore for HMCo. 6–7: Ken Karp for HMCo. 7: Ken Karp for HMCo. 10: Ken Karp for HMCo. 14: © 2000 Thomas Raupach/Woodfin Camp & Associates. 16: Ken Karp for HMCo. 17: Ken Karp for HMCo. 18: Ken Karp for HMCo. 23: *l.* E.R. Degginger/Color-Pic, Inc.; *r.* Science Exploratorium. 24: S. Nielsen/Imagery. 26–27: *bkgd.* Bob McKeever/Tom Stack & Associates; *inset* Billy Hustace. 27: © Dave

Archer/Space Art, San Rafael, California. 28: Grant Huntington for HMCo. 29: Grant Huntington for HMCo. 31: Grant Huntington for HMCo. 32: *t.l.* Grant Huntington for HMCo.; *t.r.* Grant Huntington for HMCo.; *b.* Grant Huntington for HMCo. 34: Ulf E. Wallin/The Image Bank. 36: Grant Huntington for HMCo. 37: *l.* Grant Huntington for HMCo.; *r.* Grant Huntington for HMCo. 39: Grant Huntington for HMCo. 40: *t.l.* David Young-Wolff/PhotoEdit; *t.m.* Tony Freeman/PhotoEdit; *b.l.* David Young-Wolff/PhotoEdit; *b.m.* David Young-Wolff/PhotoEdit; *b.r.* David Young-Wolff/PhotoEdit. 42: Grant Huntington for HMCo. 45: Grant Huntington for HMCo. 47: Grant Huntington for HMCo. 49: *t.* North Wind Picture Archives; *b.l.* The Granger Collection, New York; *b.r.* Stock Montage, Inc. 54: Adelina Mejia-Zelaya. 57: *t.* Ken Karp for HMCo.; *b.* Ken Karp for HMCo. 58–59: *t.* Tony Freeman/PhotoEdit; *b.* John Neubauer/PhotoEdit. 59: Peter Lambert/Tony Stone Images. 64: *t.* © 2000 Dewitt Jones/Woodfin Camp & Associates; *b.* © Lawrence Livermore/Science Photo Library/Photo Researchers, Inc. 65: *t.* Dan McCoy/Rainbow; *b.l.* Michael Newman/PhotoEdit; *b.r.* Ulrike Welsch/PhotoEdit. 66: *l.* Ken Karp for HMCo.; *r.* Ken Karp for HMCo. 67: Ken Karp for HMCo. 70–71: Deborah Davis/PhotoEdit. 71: Russ Kinne/Comstock. 73: *t.* © Mark Boulton/Photo Researchers, Inc.; *b.* Sipa Press. 76: *t.* Tony Freeman/PhotoEdit; *b.l.* Tony Freeman/PhotoEdit; *b.r.* Tony Freeman/PhotoEdit. 77: Russ Kinne/Comstock.

Unit E 1: Olaf Veltman/Creative Management Partners. 2–3: Olaf Veltman/Creative Management Partners. 4–5: *bkgd.* Michael A. Dwyer/Stock Boston; *inset* F. Scott Schafer/Outline Press Syndicate, Inc. 10: Richard Hutchings. 16: Grant Huntington for HMCo. 17: Grant Huntington for HMCo. 20: *l.* Tony Freeman/PhotoEdit; *r.* Wes Thompson/The Stock Market. 21: *t.* M.L. Sinibaldi/The Stock Market; *m.* Blaine Harrington III/The Stock Market; *b.* Jeff Gnass/The Stock Market. 24–25: *bkgd.* E.R. Degginger/Color-Pic, Inc. 26: Grant Huntington for HMCo. 27: Grant Huntington for HMCo. 29: *r.* Grant Huntington for HMCo. 31: Grant Huntington for HMCo. 32: Jeff Greenberg/PhotoEdit. 35: Grant Huntington for HMCo. 37: Grant Huntington for HMCo. 38: *l.* Daniel Brody/Stock Boston; *r.* © Jules Bucher/Photo Researchers, Inc. 39: *l.* Jan A. Zysko/NASA-KSC; *r.* © Stephen J. Krasemann/Photo Researchers, Inc. 40: *l.* Tony Stone Images; *r.* Mark Antman/Stock Boston. 41: Craig Aurness/Corbis. 42: Grant Huntington for HMCo. 43: Grant Huntington for HMCo. 44: *t.* Archive Photos; *b.* Fujifotos/The Image Works Incorporated. 45: *t.* © 2000 Juha Jormanainen/Woodfin Camp & Associates; *m.* © W. Bacon/Photo Researchers, Inc.; *b.* © 2000 Eastcott/Momatiuk/Woodfin Camp & Associates. 48: *t.r.* Jim Ballar/Tony Stone Images; *b.l.* © Syd Greenberg/Photo Researchers, Inc.; *b.r.* © Arvil A. Daniels/Photo Researchers, Inc.; *inset* © Photographics/Photo Researchers, Inc. 50: Courtesy, Anton Seimon. 50–51: *bkgd.* NASA; *inset* Courtesy, Anton Seimon. 53: Richard Hutchings for HMCo. 54: *l.* NOAA; *r.* NOAA/NESDIS/NCDC/SDSD. 55: Anthony Edgeworth/The Stock Market. 57: *l.* Gary Withey/Bruce Coleman Incorporated; *r.* Buff Corsi/Tom Stack & Associates. 59: Richard Hutchings for HMCo. 61: *l.* © NASA/Science Source/Photo Researchers, Inc.; *r.* © NOAA/Photo Researchers, Inc. 63: Ray Soto/The Stock Market. 65: Richard Hutchings for HMCo. 66–67: William Wantland/Tom Stack & Associates. 68–69: David Dennis/Tom Stack & Associates. 69: *l.* T.A. Wiewandt/DRK Photo; *r.* T.A. Wiewandt/DRK Photo. 70: *t.* NOAA/NEDIS/NCDC/SDSD; *m.* NOAA/NEDIS/NCDC/SDSD; *b.* NOAA/NEDIS/NCDC/SDSD. 72: *l.* Merilee Thomas/Tom Stack & Associates; *m.* Merilee Thomas/Tom Stack & Associates; *r.* Merilee Thomas/Tom Stack & Associates. 74–75: *bkgd.* Dewitt Jones/Corbis-Bettmann; *border* Morning Star Gallery; *r. inset* Superstock. 78: *l.* Terry Wild. 82: Richard Hutchings for HMCo. 83: Richard Hutchings for HMCo. 88: North Museum, Franklin & Marshall/Runk/Schoenberger/Grant Heilman Photography, Inc. 89: *l.* © James L. Amos/Photo Researchers, Inc.; *r.* © J.G. Paren/Science Photo Library/Photo Researchers, Inc. 90: *l.* William Johnson/Johnson's Photography; *r.* William Johnson/Johnson's Photography. 91: *t.* Anna E. Zuckerman/Tom Stack & Associates; *b.* © George Ranalli/Photo Researchers, Inc. 92: *t.* Cary Wolinsky/Stock Boston; *b.* Rob Crandall/Stock Boston.

Glossary 19: Buff Corsi/Tom Stack & Associates. 25: E.R. Degginger/Color-Pic, Inc. 31: Gary Withey/Bruce Coleman Incorporated.